BERRIGAN

BERRIGAN

a novel
by

Ginger Lox

the Naiad Press inc.
1978

Cover design by Tee A. Corinne

ISBN: 0-930044-09-6
Library of Congress Catalog Card Number 78-59620

An excerpt from BERRIGAN appeared in
SINISTER WISDOM NO. 6, SUMMER, 1978

GINGERLOX is a displaced Kansan who lives and writes in Denver, Colorado. She rarely mentions that she taught school or that her first poem was published in Teen Life in 1967. Her other early writings—poetry, editorials and articles—have appeared sporadically in such diverse publications as an oil industry bulletin, a local N.O.W. newsletter, Big Mama Rag and an anthology in Pittsburgh, Texas.

Although she is struggling into feminist consciousness, she is admittedly middle class, monogamous, and melodramatic. She had vowed to end the agony of writing fiction with this novel. Unable to resist inventing plots, however, she is now hard at work on her second book. Her friends tell her to stop worrying and quit taking herself too seriously. Her hobbies include riding the bus, pistol shooting, creating collages, paying bills and contemplating separatism.

Dedication

Berrigan is dedicated to my Sisters, all the women who have shown me who I am and what I can become.

Especially:

Janie, my very best friend, whose love gave my vision reality.

Layla, my loyal comforter.

Susie, for giving me the space to start the book.

Sandia, Eileen, Roberta, and others in the poetry group for the encouragement to write in prose.

Chocolate (who put me on the cover of her first book), who told me I should stop emulating other writers and write like myself.

Mary (who is a decent Pisces and a loyal pal but who is not good at keeping me from spending money or getting fat), who suffered through a badly copied and corrected version of the novel but who said, "Get the thing done!" and so I did.

Barbara G. and Sarah A., for their faith, support, and meticulous care in helping me bulldoze through the final rewrite.

Sappho, and the poetry of her life; *Judith Shakespeare,* denied her chance in her time, and *Rita Mae,* who paved the way and gave me words for survival.

And most of all, to all the women I have yet to meet, for in their friendship and my exchange with them lies the potential for the most worthy stories yet written.

gingerlox

Chapter 1

Every day Berrigan greets herself in her dimestore mirror, hails her own image surrounded by a brown plastic frame: *"Hello there! How's the best lesbian face I know?!"* Then she dives into a collection of clothing once worn by revolutionary spirits, though now resembling Salvation Army best. But to Berrigan, comfort is the ultimate fashion.

"Oh, to be in vogue once again!" she yawns, Daisy-ish, Fitzgerald-ish, winking in the mirror at beloved blue jeans. Yet Berrigan carries her trademarks on the inside.

(Whistle while you work, always whistle while you work) Berrigan sings to herself, in mind-radio music, a thought accompanying those efforts of trivia required to keep a household livable. Reviving tousled bed and abandoned garments, she does a bebop dish washing, taps out scooby-doo on a pan lid. The salt and pepper are in the middle of the table, her placemats washed and pressed, all the corners flat. Once again, all's well with Berrigan's world.

"Bye abode. Bye mirror. See you later, alligator. After awhile, crocodile!"

This is Berrigan today. Unafraid to be a child, she skips, the music of her mind again singing her thoughts like a wonky radio:

(Gwan to see the man,
Gwan up home.
Gwan to see the man
Who picks me like a bone.)

Berrigan is making a pilgrimage familiar to so many lesbian daughters, a social game known as "Visiting the Folks." It becomes Question and Answer time; the commentators play for blood, with the Player's Booth a locked sweatbox, a torturous coffin filled by the gas of guilt. But Berrigan will not be guilty; she loves herself and her love. She relies on her own truths.

Up the cobblestones to brownstone front door, the porch steps of home, where the remnants of a swing set rust in the front yard, bent to half-mast. *Home,* a word as warm as Christmas, spawning images tangible, touchable: faces over steaming turkey, the clink of silverware and china, jokes late at night, measured sighs when the house settles for sleep, the crisp snap of Dad's newspaper, Mom humming down the hall, everyone tangled up in tree lights trying to find the one missing bulb, the soft slap of bottom pats, a razor buzzing. And now for Berrigan knocking at this door, there is also

1

an unwritten meaning of home, etched invisibly over the arch of the door by the people who live here, the family that Berrigan comes from: *"Whosoever shall enter this portal seeks a reckoning, and possibly the hellfires of damnation!"* Berrigan chuckles. She supplies her own reckoning, in a pact with God that they both keep on truckin'.

"Welcome, welcome, prodigal!" her parents exclaim. Dad relights his pipe and Mom offers her a hug. Everyone is grinning. Berrigan's smiles are deeper; she knows what is expected.

"I hope your dogs aren't getting too fat."

"Are you locking your doors at night?"

'Need any money?"

"Are you eating right?"

Berrigan's response pacifies, shuts them out: *"Ok, Ok. Everything is Ok."*

"Why don't you come home more often, dear? We love to have you, and after all, you live so close."

The mind-radio replies, on frequencies the parents do not hear:

(Because because, endlessly because you want a "good" girl, not your gay daughter. And I can't explain to you how desperately I need to be myself as much as possible.)

The parents ask again: "Why don't you bring more of your girlfriends by?"

(Because you insult them by asking, "Why isn't a nice girl like you married?" They usually are—married to each other or to their own free identities.)

"Have you seen Evelyn lately?"

"Yes. She was by last night. She starts state CPA exams in several weeks." (And mother, I didn't fail to notice your raised eyebrows. Are you faithfully tabulating in a neat ledger: Topic, Berrigan. Headings: Time Spent With Women, Time Spent With Men. Mother, will you ever believe what your totals tell you?)

"Another of your classmates got married. That nice boy from Hartford. What was his name?"

"Gene Rally?"

"Yes, yes, that's it! Third year med, wasn't he? And did you hear that Elaine Parker got a job teaching at Antioch? Have you given any thought to going back to school, Berrigan?"

"No. You know I really don't want to do that right now. I'm enjoying my work." (School is mostly for you anyway. I don't need it now. I'm content being me, working at what I do that makes me happy.)

And then the final question from Dad, issued with a heavy sigh: "So how is your work?"

(My work, running "Shop Desiderata" where I create forms in pottery. You think it's insignificant. "Hippy trivia," wasn't that what you called it? I remember that confrontation well, when I

bought the shop. *"How can you make a decent living selling baubles?" You were both outraged. I remember. But* Decent *is a word we define differently. To you it's a secure four-figure salary that good daughters earn teaching or nursing, or keeping house for a faithful husband. To me,* Decency *is simple; you even taught it to me. Be true to yourself. Do what makes you happy.)*
"My work is fine. It's Ok. Everything is Ok. Listen, I have to go. Give Grandpa my best. Be well. Take care. I've got to go meet Evelyn at the coffee house. To help her study for exams."
"You think she'll really go to work as an accountant? We figured maybe she'd be pregnant by now. They've been married over a year. Oh well, be sure and give her our best. So long for now. Come back soon. And bring a friend!"
(Bring a friend. Preferably a man? Why don't you ever say what you mean?)
With her hand on the door handle, Berrigan looks at her parents with the light from the living room behind them, leaves them, *"Bye Bye Bye,"* and then, calling back to them from the street: *"Don't walk under any squeaky ladders!"*
Her father's answer comes with her mother's wave: "Don't take any wooden nickels!"
Now Berrigan's mind-radio goes again, running like her smiles, on secrets passed in dreams by former seers, full of passions and perceptions unrestrained, uncommon:
(Up and saw the man
Living on the hill.
Up and saw the man
Whose heart is never still.
Ho hum a holiday
Ho hum a holiday
La la la.)

* * * * * *

Berrigan today came out of a yesterday woman formed by time spent in self-search often enlightening, sometimes a nightmare. She arrives upon her now-ness knowing that learning is scary and terrific: losing self to gain self, stumbling in darkness to round a corner into bright light and clear passage, gasping at the luck of surviving. Telling about the yesterday Berrigan is as important as describing her present identity. Her travels in and out of the lives of others have determined who she has become. Women along the way helped. Each gave her a clue that brought her one step closer to herself. If Berrigan were a butterfly, then these women helped costume her for that eventual arrival, that monumental cocoon-bursting. Each added a special color to her wings, painted more carefully than a cathedral window.
One of the first women to guide the yesterday, early-growing Berrigan was Doris Shelby, whose job at the local Family Counsel-

3

ing Center was mostly that of "professional listener." Doris's successes with young people were easily traceable to the way she dealt with them.

At the time Doris and Berrigan met, Berrigan was feeling the pressures of adolescence, being a young lesbian in Bingham, Connecticut, with no one to talk to. She had been carrying her feelings around like secrets in hip pockets. When the pockets overflowed, Berrigan stepped out of the neurotic masses and into the door of the counseling center. As for the atmosphere awaiting her, blue rugs and potted plants alleviated any hints of padded-cell decor. Indeed, Berrigan was quite surprised on her first meeting with Doris at seeing how much Doris looked like anyone else. *(Here's Doris, quite unlike I imagined. Where are the coke-bottle glasses, the thick-soled shoes, the clinical white coat? My God, I'm about to pour my lesbian heart out to Loretta Young!)*

But it wasn't that traumatic. Berrigan is an easy friend. "Relax," Doris told her new client, putting up both hands in front of her. "I hold no mean mind-machine upon my person!"

Berrigan's response came in a gush of openness. She was not a student of guile nor a willing procrastinator. And she had come to the Center earnestly seeking help.

Berrigan: *"Is it my turn for an introduction?"* Doris: "Only if you want to give me one. But canned speeches are not required."

"I guess I'm here for a whole lot of reasons: confusion, frustration, even because I'm scared maybe. I need your advice or whatever else you dole out here so that I don't feel so isolated in dealing with things. Mostly I need to be told my problems aren't dumb. I can't seem to find anyone I know to talk to that I trust enough to understand my point of view. So I guess a stranger might be the best listener. But look, first there's something that I want to tell you so I don't have to double-talk around it. Well . . . . I never said this right out to anyone but . . . . I'm a lesbian. I've been with several women already in the past two years. My parents don't know. But I'm not here to be cured for that. As far as I'm concerned, being lesbian is not what's bugging me most."

"That's quite an opener to tell a stranger."

"Does it bother you?"

"No. Does it bother you?"

"Maybe not being able to talk about it is what bothers me."

"Well, I'm sure as hell glad you're not just another hostile youth!" Doris said, grinning.

And Berrigan answered with one of her own deeper smiles. The first hurdle was over.

"Where do we go from here?"

"Let's relax and talk for a start."

"What? No couch? No tape recorder? No hidden cameras? No two-way mirror window?"

"Nope, none of those. Just you and me, face to face."

4

* * * * * *

Berrigan was unafraid of revealing her problems and opinions to Doris.

"I look at the world, both inside and outside Bingham; it's so depressing, but I don't know what to do. Every time I watch the news, I get all stirred up. There are a million needy people, each with a desperate cause. Where can I be the most help? Everyone at school laughs at me. 'You're too serious, Berrigan. There's nothing you can do anyway,' they tell me. My parents say, 'Your time will come! Just be patient! The world isn't so bad as it seems. You may learn to view it in a different way when you're older.' But the older I get, Doris, the more concerned I get."

Doris was surprised at the depth of Berrigan's consideration for more than herself and local activities. She was a poetic spirit, a young philosopher, a rare idealist in starkly realistic times. And Doris saw this as a great gift, a reviving energy contrasted to the cynicism, hedonism, and apathy evident in many of her other young clients. Accordingly, she responded to Berrigan in special terms. Doris concluded after ten weeks of meetings: "Berrigan, you're suffering from 'poetic aphonia.' "

"What's that? It sounds illegal! Is it contagious?"

"Berrigan, you're full of pity and compassion for the world broiling around you. You suffer in learning this is not America the Beautiful. The streets are full of faces of agony: people crippled, starving, haunted, lonely, old, drunks, addicts. We cast them out of our lives if they belong to us, hoping they'll stay away. Yet many of them bring their misery upon themselves. You can't shelter them or show them a better way; experts have tried and usually failed. You've got to learn to accept that you can't bring in every lame cat! You can't try to carry a universal pain inside of you and hope to survive. Even Jesus had help! I know you can't ignore the people around you who are hurt, searching, lost. You're too sensitive and caring a person to do that. But you need to remember too that you have to take care of Number One, yourself. You do the best you can, but you take care of you too. It's all right to be selfish; you earn the right to be that way by giving the best you've got and admitting when there's no more to draw from. No one else will take care of you, I assure you. We're all too involved in our own crises. Only by doing this will you prevent yourself from joining the faces of agony. And even more important, you can't help anyone else until you know how to help yourself."

"I guess you think I'm trying to be Joan of Arc, huh?"

"More like Wonderwoman maybe. No, Berrigan, your idealism is not only natural but admirable. I never even thought to worry about the world when I was your age; I was too busy biting my nails and wondering if Joe Eddy Peabody would notice me."

"Did he?"

"Luckily he didn't. I didn't know it then, but he wasn't my type. He's now on a long vacation in Folsom Prison!"

And then, during their eleventh meeting:

"I had a nightmare last night that scared me."

"Can you describe it?"

"It's future time, like about 2085. At first what I see is from a distance. I am staring at acres of cement, from one horizon to the other. Then I can see closer; there are two huge circles painted on the cement, one blue and the other red. A wildly gesticulating man at a lectern is giving a speech to thousands of children. All the little boys are standing in the red circle, with all the little girls standing in the blue one. I cannot hear the speech, can only see the grotesque delivery of the man at the lectern. Suddenly he stops talking and moving. All the children turn together to face me. They begin to move toward me, walking slowly and stiffly. I see that the girls all wear aprons and carry spatulas in their left hands. The boys each have a short whip, and their boots snap on the cement as they march in unison. All their faces wear plastic smiles, and they move steadily towards me, these lines of children marching within the boundaries of their colored circles.

"Nothing else happened in the dream because suddenly everything is on fire: it all disappeared in a hot crackling, like a film clip burned in a projector. I woke up terrified, hot and cold at the same time. All I could think of was those empty faces in that cold world totally without personal choice. I was afraid the dream would become real, not in 2085, but tomorrow, when the sun came out."

"And how do you feel now?"

"Still a little shaky."

"Do you really believe the dream could come true, now as we're together discussing it?"

"No . . . . but I guess it was symbolic of my feelings about society. Yeah, I think that was what the dream was about: how frustrating it is to be role-ized from the time you're small—your parents programing you to grow up to be a good female robot with the proper female robot behavior."

"What about male robots? Or is the programing one-sided?"

"I wonder about the reality of freedom, seeing the social condition thrive on victimization, but somehow I don't see men suffering from it as much as women. They're robotized too, but they have the short whips at least, something to use as a weapon. It just seems to me that they don't have it so bad.

"What I feel most after the dream and in general is futility. I know I'm a feminist, by intuition more than any education. And I think these feelings are tied directly to my attitudes about men and roles and my own female robot programing. The whole sex scene is an intense phasma, boiling inside of me, knotting my stomach up. I'm doubled over inside, but I can't seem to deal with the phasma so that I can stand upright without the pain."

6

"Have you tried to contact any other feminists here in Bingham?"

"I'm not much into organizations and that's where most of the feminists here seem to be. I just can't get into the group rap thing right now. At this point, I'm very cautious about trusting and so I'm not secure about hanging my life out for view to anyone. Actually, the reason I don't fit well into groups is probably because I think attitudes can only be changed on a one-to-one level. It's just that I get so full of my own emotions that everything I say ends up a pitiful garble. I'm worn out with always being in someone's 'territory,' being scanned and judged as open game. Yet most of my friends don't seem to notice. They act like I'm crazy, or worse, some kind of traitor. But I just can't accept the lack of respect men generally show for women, or the idea that I deserve insults and derision just for popping out female and refusing to be ashamed of that. I should probably be more assertive but I don't know how. I can't march or carry signs or make grand speeches; it's not in my nature. All I've got at this point is a gut full of anger and no words."

Perhaps the most useful session for both women came near the end of Berrigan's therapy. Doris said, "I'd like to begin today's discussion with a simple question: 'Do you hate men?' "

For a moment, Berrigan's brain jangled with an angry wave.

(Dum de dum dum! The $64,000 question! And what will follow if I say yes? A diagnosis of the "Bad dyke" syndrome, questions that haunt homosexual dreams? "Is your hairdresser a fag?" "Did you ride horses as a child?" "Were you a tomboy?" "Do you love your father?" "Are you afraid of penises?" "Do you hate your father?" Were you or weren't you breastfed?" "Do you remember if you liked it?" "Was your potty-training difficult?" "Are you a cucumber fetishist?" "Do you covet a motorcycle?" blah blah blah blah)

"Well, Berrigan?" Doris was unrelenting, but not righteous. Berrigan relaxed.

"I don't suppose I like men much. Actually, it's 'Maleness' or what a 'Real Man' is supposedly like that makes me mad. All this 'Macho' mania. I don't think I'm a man-hater. Men as a whole affect me with their disrespect and their arrogance, but on a personal level, I am not intimate with men. I cannot get close to them. They cannot get close to my heart. All the guys I've known seem like stick-figures to me, shadows without souls.

"With Arby, everything was 'Jivo!' He was possessed with being 'Hip' and soon left me for a real live-in.

"Joel told me, 'Berrigan, you are incredible!' and I was impressed.

"Raphael completely disproved all myths about Latin lovers.

"Ray, Ray Purty . . . senior class president, leader on the honor roll, was a very serious young man. He wanted to get married, would have harnessed me with an apron and a playpen full of miniatures just like him.

7

"Lee played guitar for me by candlelight, and left beard-burns on my chin. There were a few more . . . they all left small burns in me somehow, tiny aches I could never define or quench, fire flickers. Now they're just ashes, these impressions of the men in my life.

"And now for a few words on the women I've known. Equal time, you know!

"Women are less defensive lovers. My best girlfriend in high school, Nonnie, was the most vulnerable, giving person I ever met. She never felt the need to explain her affection for me. She kissed me one Sunday afternoon, on her bed, with the pep club pom-pons in our school hanging above us. I suppose the wind of guilt should have swept in on me then, but it didn't. Every time I saw those orange and black pom-pons shake at school rallies, I remembered her kiss. The feelings were good. I read Orlando *when I was a senior and thought I'd burst with admiration for Virginia Woolf. I moped for days about the injustices which caused her suicide. 'History is such a boor!' I proclaimed, 'Just pages full of destruction and conquering of so many centuries of warriors.' I didn't learn about the Amazon warriors, the earth mothers. Those matriarchal societies were totally ignored in my courses. I committed a dreadful social crime in observing how much of Attila The Hun was evident in some of the school football heroes. Bingham High was not impressed with my sense of historic indignation.*

"But my English teacher, Adrienne Dulcea, encouraged me, telling me: 'Sometimes I think you're the only free thinker in my class. Somewhere along the line you didn't abandon your imagination.' When Keats wrote about the lovers frozen at the point of consummation on the grecian urn, I could feel their agony. Everyone else in class just thought he was a dumb Englishman preoccupied with writing poems to a vase. Out of their ignorance came crude satires aimed at Keats: 'Ode to a pickled lobster,' 'Ode to a fancy fern,' 'Ode to my sweatsock,' and so on. And I wonder where my indignation began! Of course, I was in love with Dulcea, because she introduced me to my first passion: Literature. I remember being spellbound at her descriptions of those authors I came to love: Woolf, Colette, Stein, Dickinson. She was the first really proud woman I knew.

"I spent three summers holding hands in the woods with Carole, counselor at Camp Onahoogie. The ornery girls she taught so patiently to canoe would have found us a great comedy if they had seen us head-to-head by our campfire, listening to the sounds of the trees and the wind. Of all that I have learned from women, Carole was the most in touch with the earth. 'Every stone has a song,' she told me, 'And every turning moon a new promise.' We discovered love-making together, and so were not afraid. I was no catch then, all nerve endings and straggly hair. But she encouraged me, with a confidence that never wavered. Inside of me lived a brilliant butterfly, the colors of the rainbow. Carole never doubted the cocoon

8

would fall away, and the better creature would appear.

"Beverly, the daughter of the tenants on my Uncle David's farm, used to climb into the loft with me and we would yell out against the age-soaked beams: 'We are queer, we are queer!'

"Sharon Blessing, the minister's eldest, used to to rip my buttoms off in passionate handfuls, as we sat at the back of Buster's moviehouse.

"And then there was my favorite cousin Jo, who smelled like lilacs and chocolate, whose elbows and knees were never sharp. Her back was bronze in starlight.

"These are the women I have known, parts of them that I loved carried in me like lucky pieces."

"I think you have some of the answers to your own questions now, Berrigan. How do you feel about the sessions we've been having?"

"Oh, I know there aren't going to be any overnight changes, but I guess it's still what I want. It's my recurrent fantasy, but I think you've convinced me that it's ok to have the fantasy as long as I don't get impatient. I know I'm waiting for the womanworld to occur in one fell swoop, and yet if it did, I wouldn't be ready for it, couldn't help it evolve. I'm still tongue-tied, I guess, by the enormous 'ruling male phantom.' "

"Berrigan, just remember: no man can really take anything away from you unless you let yourself be baited. You can always go home whole, no matter what they say or do, if you let them know their arrogance is irrelevant to you and only reflects on them. Actually, sometimes silence is a good weapon; it dissipates conflict and confuses an oppressor. But above all, don't be afraid to trust yourself, Berrigan. You have your answers, and they will be accessible, if you give yourself time and experience in developing them. Then maybe you'll be able to extend to others in a way that gives you more confidence. And don't be afraid to ask for help—especially from another woman!"

"And the shrink declared: Live your love instead of thinking it?"

"Yes, Berrigan something like that."

"You do pretty good for a stranger."

"Well, thanks, you're not so bad yourself!"

And then, like the first day they met, Doris grinned and Berrigan answered smiling, both of them full of new contemplation, having seen in their weeks together over the horizon of strangers and into each other as friends.

Chapter 2

Berrigan began her freshman year at Bingham College with a mixture of expectation and excitement. It was during early student orientation that she encountered Linda Framer, at a Sexual Freedom rap at Dumont House on the Bingham campus. The exchange brought a mutual reaction: the women were unimpressed with each other.

They did not meet again until enrollment for fall session, when, to their dismay, they were paired together in a room at the dorm.

"Fucking selection computers," Linda growled.

"Technology fails again," Berrigan countered.

It seemed that the campus computers (used to shuffling hundreds of student registration cards) had arbitrarily designed that Linda and Berrigan spend time together, since they found themselves in four of the same classes. Linda soon demonstrated that she was not in college for any scholastic motives. She pitted herself against everyone and everything, especially Berrigan, as if entirely committed to destroying all egos and all sanity in the process. In addition, she tried to compete with every other female in her classes, by jiggly exposures of cleavage and legs. Bitchy, flirty, Hartford born-and-bred, she let her body be her only advertising.

Meanwhile back at the dorm, her attack continued on a grander scale. Driving large nails into the wall at both ends of the room and then attaching a sturdy rope, Linda hung a blanket over this. She had improvised an effective division of the room, and significantly stated her feelings about her roommate. They were the talk of the dorm: "Go down to Room 620 and have a look at the 'Berlin Blanket!' " For Berrigan, the entire situation was agonizing. She was used to relating easily to people, used to liking others and being liked for herself. She thought withdrawing from people was wrong, but so was delving into them or demanding their attention. She had tried her best to be pleasant to Linda, despite the obvious personality conflict. Linda's anti-Berrigan campaign was not only distressing, but it was an even deeper worry because Berrigan was eager to break out of distrusting women. But any discussions of women's issues or feminist campus group activities only brought a look of snobbish disdain from Linda. As a result, Berrigan kept her ideas under wraps, unexposed.

Night after night, lying in her bed on her side of the "Berlin

Blanket," Berrigan tried to recall something she'd said or done to insult Linda, to bring about this unceasing conflict between them. But actually, she'd never had a chance! From the moment they headed for door 620 and realized their destination was the same, war was unofficially declared. Where had it all started? Vaguely, Berrigan redrew the scene at Dumont House, their first meeting.

Donated to the campus by a church in Bingham, Dumont House served as a student lounge. On Fridays, the main room was turned into an expresso house and an open forum for poets, musicians, interpretive dance programs, amateur soap-box speakers. For several years, Bingham College had sponsored a lecture series called "Controversy Today." Speakers were invited to BC to speak to the student assembly: a group of radical anti-Viet Nam poets, civil rights leaders, several feminist writers, and the leading psychologist in violence therapy. Frequently, the guest lecturers stopped by Dumont House after their speeches to rap and meet students at close range.

On the particular night Berrigan had first seen Linda, she'd gone to Dumont House to hear a lecture in the "Sexual Freedom" category of the C.T. series. Speaking was an up-and-coming lesbian writer, Ann Turley. Not only was her novel uninhibited in its lesbian theme, but Turley herself remained unruffled by disapproving hecklers in the crowd—many of them secret voyeurs aching to watch two women making love. But as she put it, "The book is selling, isn't it?" When someone suggested, "Only queers are buying it!" she came back with, "Oh really? I didn't know any of them could read. I thought all they did was molest children."

The coffee house was unusually packed; Turley had won over the few overt gays on campus, intrigued the latent roommates and jock closet-queens, equally incensing the crewcut athletes and "Jesus freaks." She came to Dumont House after her speech even though she was unsure of any support. Berrigan admired her courage, her chutzpah.

The crowd of students fragmented into cliques, buzzing with many different tones of opinion. Yet the energy of suppressed anger was stifling, a confrontation surely brewing. It was then that Berrigan caught sight of Linda in a crowd of couples; she was leaning against a far wall, a perfect "Suzy Sorority," head slightly back, her cigarette poised.

As Berrigan recalled, there had been some harassing comments directed at Turley, many from the fraternity boys and athletes in Linda's crowd. But finally the students sitting blankly moon-faced and silent began to animate. The "proud dyke" became less a freakish anomaly and more a relaxed artist discussing her difference. Living as a social renegade for years, Turley knew how to answer ignorance without much contest. Hesitant questions emerged from the students and gradually the atmosphere grew comfortable as many topics were touched upon. Everyone, even the initially skeptical, enjoyed Turley's openness and willingness to use irony to poke fun at the stereotypes and misconceptions which plague lesbians.

The last issue discussed that evening was bisexuality and Berrigan had contributed some remarks. It was her guess that bisexuality was probably more widespread than any statistics estimated, in view of the campus climate of sexual experimentation. She remembered trying to be witty: *"It's even likely that some couples here tonight are dealing with a bisexual situation. Maybe it's another woman she goes to meet when she leaves you!"*

And then the lightbulb: an idea popped into Berrigan's mind, popped out of the scene she was mentally recreating. *(Maybe that's it! The remark I made about some of the couples dealing with bisexuality!)*

If Linda was struggling with bisexual feelings, or had had a bisexual experience that her lover knew about, maybe *this* was the source of her hostility. Berrigan knew just from observing Linda with her friends that while she appeared to be a showcase of seduction, she was not a coquette. She did not have a passive mind; she had a demanding nature and an intense temper. The boys she traveled with wanted her, but not her caustic tongue, her emphatic opinions. Linda had been with Gene Rally the night of Turley's lecture, and they had had fierce words and left shortly after the discussion on bisexuality. Berrigan hoped she had found the key. She could cope better with the thought that Linda's hate campaign was not directed at her personally, but only at her as a symbol of Linda's own divided sexuality. She hoped she could convince her roommate that she was not a threat to her.

But before Berrigan had a chance to give her idea any further speculation, Linda and Gene burst into the dark dorm room. In drunken voices they were arguing, laughing, shuffling and stumbling. The night table fell over against Berrigan's bed, snagging the divider blanket. Then the two of them fell in a heap of squeaking springs onto Linda's bed.

"You clumsy bastard," Linda groaned, "get off me!"

"Come on, Linda. Come on, let me love you."

"Love me, my ass!"

"Well then, give me your ass!"

Amidst more raucous laughter, Linda's semi-struggles grew less intense and Gene's advances more amorous. From her neighboring bedside, Berrigan was bewildered and furious with them, partly because if Gene was discovered in their room, Berrigan could be hauled on the carpet for Linda's indiscretion. Then Linda said, "You don't make much noise, do you, Gene?"

"Silent studs, us Tau Kay Epsilons!"

"Bedroom bullshitters, more likely. Come on, Gene. Open the throttle. I want to hear your engine really running!"

"Jesus Linda, it's true. You are all mouth!"

12

But their disagreement got no further because the lights came on, blinding them both. The blanket divider suddenly snapped down, plaster chips flying as the rope gave way and the nails pulled out of the wall. Berrigan was standing looking at them, flushed with anger, the rope and part of the blanket crumpled in her hand. She told Gene to get out. He left without grace, backing from the room as he pulled at his belt and zipped his pants hastily. Linda raised up on the bed, shielding her eyes from the light.

"The campaign is over, Linda. You and Gene just blew it."

"Roll over, baby dyke, and mind your own business."

They gauged each other for a moment, neither of them moving.

(How drunk is she?)

("How mad is she?")

"Just tell me one thing, Linda. For whose benefit was Gene's 'noise' supposed to be? I don't really believe you find his 'sounds of passion' exciting."

"What the fuck are you talking about?"

"The jig is up, Linda, and I'm not even sure you know it. These months of agony have had very little to do with me personally. You're just uptight because I'm a lesbian and you think you'd like to try it. Maybe you already have, and Gene has the idea you want something extra going on in this dorm room that doesn't include him. Well, I've paid a helluva price for your conflict, and now I've had it."

Linda was sobering, but so far unargumentative.

"Bringing Gene in here tonight finally tied up the connection that I've been scouring my conscience for all this time. You remembered what I said about bisexuality at Dumont House when Ann Turley was here, as if my remarks were personal accusations aimed at you and Gene. I don't know what's hanging you up, but the efforts you've made trying to prove yourself exclusively heterosexual by crucifying me have been monumentally ridiculous. Revving up the motors in the bed next door epitomizes that. Do you really believe that my overhearing Gene as a notorious hump proves anything to either of us?"

"What would you know about it? You think heterosexuality is Yellowstone Kelly fucking a bear."

"And how would you know what I think? You've never spoken to me enough to know if I even talk, much less about Yellowstone Kelly, heterosexuality, or anything else. All you know about me is what you've heard and what your own prejudices have construed. You've never even called me by my name."

All Linda offered at this point was her silence, and a stare out from under a rapidly vanishing stupor.

"Whether you go or stay in this room is irrelevant to me. But if you stay, know this: the 'Berlin Blanket' is permanently down."

Berrigan righted the nightstand, knowing her rush was over.

13

Linda finally seemed to understand the scope of the incident.

"Why didn't you say anything sooner? Why didn't you protest? Why did you put up with me?"

"I didn't know you. I didn't have a clue about you or your anger towards me until tonight. I can't use myself as a weapon, Linda. I'm overwhelmed by attack. Besides, how could I defend myself from an invisible, unspoken charge? Contrary to common gossip, dykes have feelings too."

"So what have you been feeling that you wouldn't say?"

"Futility, Linda. Mine has had one helluva good look at yours."

* * * * * *

If fantasy had won out, the next night Linda would have crawled into Berrigan's bed, whispering her roommate's name for the first time, and their herstory as lovers would have begun. But the months of distance and bitterness could only dissolve gradually. Berrigan was willing to exchange the effort of friendship. What were grudges but useless baggage for the soul? And besides, only a fool would let Linda remain an enemy. Berrigan was neither angel nor fool; while Linda slowly emerged, Berrigan kept her faith. Inside her head, songs of hope were humming; she was also ignoring that warning that had appeared in her mind when she first set eyes on Linda. Lame cats come in all disguises; Berrigan could not seem to recognize the camouflage in Linda's case, or else she was forgetting to listen to herself.

The two women had few similar interests; their choice of friends was completely opposite. Linda thrived on the jazzy camaraderie of the coffee house where the boys were full of beer and quick to laugh, the girls were no competition, no threat to her. To Berrigan, the coffee house was a shallow place, a den full of shadows. The faces full of needs were too blatant and depressing. There was no one-to-one contact, only bodies bumping like pinballs, making blind scores. Berrigan enjoyed a smaller, more careful selection of friends, in particular two female classmates. Trudy and Susan had lived together since their freshman year, and were established as Bingham's in-residence "lesbian couple." They were seniors now, wiser older company for Berrigan to keep, yet bright and hopeful like her. Their company was comfortable, the greatest recommendation in Berrigan's code. The threesome played bridge, caught the flicks at the Strand, frisbied in the park, and rapped for hours into the night, postulating on women's politics, creating their own "Controversy Today" speeches.

The Blanket had come down and the cannons were stowed, but it seemed that the Cold War had set in. Berrigan and Linda were seldom in the room at the same time; the computers had pulled a reverse and so they had no second semester courses together. Linda kept late hours and Berrigan often spent nights and weekends with Trudy and Susan. It took a situation as vague as the one at

Dumont House to finally stir fantasy closer to realization.

After the flicks one Friday night, Berrigan and her friends went to their favorite student restaurant in Bingham-proper. "BJ's" was one of the few places off-campus with two alluring aspects: low rates (especially on Pizza Supreme) and a pro-student owner, Joe DiMona. Joe was not like the other businessmen in town, who lived in the fear that Bingham College would any day become a second Berkeley and cringed if students tried to become regular customers. On that same night, all the frat boys and their coterie of female admirers, with Linda reigning, were on the way to BJ's after deciding, "The beer taps are faster there!"

As usual, the frat set announced their arrival rudely, barging into the private moods of people at different tables. Berrigan had never understood the reasoning of this crowd; the crude remarks and haughty posing were all part of their reputation. "They're so bad!" seemed to be a compliment sought in earnest, some kind of achievement-in-reverse, an award for "Most Notably Dishonorable."

With their movie discussion shattered, the three women chose not to stay at BJ's observing Tau Kay Epsilon's well known lack of manners. As they got up from their booth, Trudy saw Linda. "Hey, Ber, isn't that your roommate?" Berrigan searched the sounds and shapes, locating Linda with Gene, necking near the jukebox. *"Yes, there she is, Miss Christian Fellowship herself."* "A picture of beauty and brains, an example for future generations!" *"Reproduction fails again?"* They shared a laugh as they collected their coats to leave.

Cobb, one of the obnoxious and vocal athletes at the Turley lecture, had always had the most bravado among the frat boys. Now his voice came through BJ's loud and clear, just as it had in assaulting Turley at Dumont House.

"Well, well, what have we in this corner here?
A queer, a queer, and another queer!
I've heard you do it on your knees,
But I never guessed you favored threes!"

Some of the other boys cheered Cobb on, like a chorus of stupid claquers glittering with the bravery of beer. Cobb lurched towards the three women, menacing:

"Oh yes, here's Bingham's dainty three.
Each a prim hard-core lesbie!
With boobies no gent shall ever squeeze,
But give *me* a chance, if you please!"

He half-ran at them, tripping on one of the stools and falling onto their table, and then onto the floor. Several of the boys tried to catch him, but could only steady themselves in the confusion. Susan held onto Trudy, who was tensing, livid. Berrigan wondered where Wonderwoman was.

"Cobb, you're an ass. What kind of a stud picks on lesbians?"

15

It was Linda. All of a sudden, no one was laughing anymore and Cobb knew he had made himself an idiot.

"He's just worried one of them will get his sister," a friend said.

"I doubt they'd want any relative of Cobb's. I wouldn't," Linda finished.

Cobb was helped up and out the door, as Joe tried to apologize to his three distressed customers. Berrigan didn't hear anything he was saying; she was watching Linda leave, with a dumbfounded Gene following.

Berrigan knew Linda had risked her approval with the frat set when she put Cobb down at BJ's. What she couldn't figure out was whether Linda had a personal hassle with Cobb or if she was beginning to empathize, beginning to deal with her own sexual feelings towards women. Or maybe Linda was just tired of the smart remarks connecting her with Berrigan, and so she decided to put a stop to it. Berrigan wanted to find out the motive for Linda's intervention on her behalf. She began to stay at the dorm, hoping she might catch Linda in for more than a few minutes. Coincidentally, Gene and Linda were arguing and so she was spending less time with him at his apartment and more time in her own room.

Looking unsuccessfully for Linda in the cafeteria one day, Berrigan found her instead sunbathing on the roof-deck outside their window. This was off-limits to the dorm women but the rule was generally ignored. A tan was always more important than a scolding from the floor supervisor.

"Are you really sunning, or just watching the muscle parade?" Berrigan asked, standing at the window, indicating the steady flow of shirtless machos strolling past the dorm, hoping to catch sight of someone half-dressed. Linda was on her stomach with her back to Berrigan.

"A little of both, I guess. Want to join me?"

"For the sun, *yes."*

Berrigan sat down by Linda, noticing several men clustered just below the deck; they seemed to have stopped and stared up in their direction when she appeared on the roof.

(Everyone on the campus must know Linda Framer is on the deck at Jensen Hall with her top unstrapped.)

"How does it feel to be the object of 650 individual lusts at Bingham College?" The comment was Berrigan's idea of a half-joke.

"How does it feel to be known as the Campus Lesbian?"

"Touché, Linda."

"Berrigan, let me ask you something. Does one of those girls . . . . belong to you?"

"Trudy and Susan? No, they belong to themselves and enjoy their freedom best with each other."

"Where's your friend?"

"I don't have a lover, if that's what you mean."

16

"You could have Gene, and that would be close enough."

Berrigan laughed. *"Why do you go with him if the two of you are so incompatible?"*

"Are we?"

"Sometimes it looks that way. I don't think you're very happy, with Gene or any of those lard-headed jocks and frat boys."

"Don't kid yourself. When I need a ride or a cheat-sheet, I get it. If I need an escort, I have one. When I'm broke and want a beer, it's there. They serve their purpose."

"But they don't serve you."

"I get out of it just what I put into it."

"I think you're the one getting put into, and for cheap returns."

"And what's my alternative? Make the three campus dykes four?"

Berrigan didn't answer because at the point, Linda turned to her and sat up, her top falling away from her breasts. It was soley for Berrigan's benefit, and she did not refuse to look at the firm bosom even Cobb would not have believed. And then in full view of the parade below and at least fifteen pairs of binoculars, Linda put her hand behind Berrigan's head, pulled her face down to her own, and kissed her. Fantasy materialized on the roof of Jensen Hall at Bingham College.

The talks that ate into the early morning hours were now between Linda and Berrigan: about Gene, ego, dreams, school. But not about love, feminism, politics, people. Berrigan was the listener while Linda monopolized her as captive audience. She told all, as if Berrigan's trust would purge the confused and guilty feelings she had been harboring since they met. Their discussions about "the guilt trip" nearly renewed the Berlin Blanket. A victim of the morality of strict parents and early religious training, Linda was convinced that any alternatives to heterosexuality were pursuits of evil. But her own double standards were unraveling before her. Her behavior toward Berrigan was an obvious indication that some of her guilt could be repressed, in her pursuit of pleasure.

Like drops of water and oil on the ocean, Berrigan and Linda floated together within the unique protected world of Bingham College, touching, yet running together without mixing. Why did Berrigan persist in a relationship with so little relevance to the one-to-oneness most important to her, a relationship that started at battle-stations? Why did she meet her roommate's innocuous terms: "Support me, lend an ear, a hand when I'm lonely or afraid, come to bed when I call you, but make no demands on me"? Berrigan was gauging all the levels and coming through to keep them balanced; Linda was sailing blind and selfish, oblivious to everything but her own ego, her own needs.

"Live your love instead of thinking it." Doris's persistent advice came to Berrigan's memory repeatedly, ringing like a gong sounding the hours of the day. She knew that was not the direction her life was taking. She was neither desperate for a lover, nor ignorant of Linda's utilizing her. Gene was still very much on the scene, although Linda's interest in him had taken a downswing. She kept him around as a power play; after all, manipulating two people was far more interesting to Linda than just one, and if either of them dumped her, there was always an alternate companion available. Linda's calculations weren't random. Berrigan and Gene both cared for her, which made all the difference. A jangled threesome they comprised, with two parties unwilling. Gene knew Berrigan was the cause for Linda's sleeping less with him, and he disliked her for that. Likewise, Berrigan knew Gene was Linda's pawn, her social escort, her "out" for acceptability. Should the situation at the dorm irritate her, she ran to him in a flurry of effective melodrama. Only Linda found emotional vitality in this ménage-à-trois; she had two sources of affection, concern, and attention. If one spotlight dimmed, there was another to keep her out of the dark. Gene's motive was sexual, despite the infrequency of their contact. Berrigan, on the other hand, had a nobler motive, one far less personally rewarding. She had succumbed to a former pitfall; the "lame cat" syndrome had her in a merciless grip. Linda needed "to be saved from herself," and Berrigan had risen to the task, even as she watched herself fall away in pieces, a victim of her own charity.

* * * * * *

The Ghia buzzed along the road like a happy ladybug, all its parts in tune, its mechanical mood unencumbered by the load of suitcases, wig boxes, and laundry Linda and Berrigan had stuffed in the trunk and backseat.

(On the road to Hartford, gwan up east.
Heart risin', dreams puffin'
Like they was laced with yeast.
Gwan to meet new parents,
Another mom and dad.
New eyes and questions:
Will my answers make them sad?
On the road to Hartford,
Gwan up east.
Wish I had a true love,
To give my heart a feast.)

What a bust, a complete bust, a tiring facade: the three-day Labor Day break wasted except for the panorama of eastern countryside in late summer dress. Linda's parents hadn't liked Berrigan from the time she said hello. It was not that she was surly or rude. She had been rejected because her face said all the words that she did not: about Linda, about the home Linda came from, and about Berrigan herself, as a creature dedicated to personal freedom.

18

Every evening, the supper table conversations became "Framer's Family Forum," and Berrigan suffered to keep her cool while Linda's father and mother exchanged ignorance on politics, people, the world. Their opinions were firm: all feminists were insane women with impotent husbands. Politicians were corrupt bastards bleeding the public's pocketbook. Jews were definitely not Robin Hood since they robbed the poor and got richer. Eldridge Cleaver was demented due to sickle cell anemia having destroyed his brain. And political terrorists deserved exactly what they got.

"It's a shame firing squads have been outlawed," Linda's father declared.

Time and again, Berrigan started to interject her own opinions, but Linda intervened in a panic. "More potatoes, Berrigan? More salad? Dessert?"

(Her parents conclude that I am a voiceless idiot with a voracious appetite. Safe, but stupid.)

Playing right into Linda's hand, Berrigan spent the time with the Framers agonizing, frustrated. The hours were awkward and uncomfortable, endless in passing. Only when they went to the basement to wash the bags full of a semester's clothes were they alone, escaping the shuffling of silent looks and nervous sounds.

"Don't say anything," Linda rasped. "They don't suspect a thing!"

Linda and her mother walked arm-in-arm to the car when the two women were ready to go back to Bingham and college.

"Take care driving back, Linda."

"Work on those grades," her father added. Then they looked at Berrigan, both of them ineffectually absent of a way to say goodbye.

Linda's mother started to extend her hand, but the gesture jerked and died midway. "Come again, Berrigan," she mumbled.

Linda's father stared at this feet. *(He must be praying for deliverance.)*

On the way back to Bingham, they argued, and then Berrigan withdrew into silence. The fantasy of love and trust had emerged for Linda in their relationship, by her selfish, half-assed evaluation. But for Berrigan, it was only a nightmare, antithetical to all she hopefully sought. Even the ultimate comfort of physical affection could not convince her to continue chasing after a "better Linda," a ghost of Berrigan's own imagination. Her own folly about saving Linda was beginning to haunt her, a painful spectre of foolishness.

Linda pulled off the road near a grove of trees and a cornfield. "Let's take a walk." Berrigan didn't answer; she sat in the car a few minutes after Linda had gone, and then followed. At first, she couldn't find her, and walked into the middle of the dense trees. A giggle startled her, then something hit her shoulder. It was Linda's blouse, and then there was Linda, standing naked in the trees,

19

beckoning Berrigan like a mischievous woodnymph.

"Some prank, Linda. But no thanks."

Berrigan's pout did not deter Linda. She came to Berrigan and embraced her, began to undress her. Let the woodnymphs become two instead of one . . . .

What would a woodsman have thought, coming upon two naked women sleeping in embrace, quiet and lost in the reverie of satiation? What would a poet say about their faces and their gentle hair, or four breasts friendly resting?

No phallus here,
My sister dear.
Just you and me
Loving free.
We need no man.
We have our hands.
Open, come, give:
Woman, lover — live.

* * * * * *

Despite Linda's efforts to distract Berrigan with spontaneous lovemaking, on waking they dressed and emerged from the trees into the same world, with the same arguments. They were still relating at crossed points, their contact empty and one-sided. Though Linda gabbed and cajoled the rest of the way back to Bingham from her parents' house, Berrigan was deaf to it, numb with confusion. Her own thoughts were sounding out too loud; they drowned Linda's aimless chatter.

(I do not choose wise Odysseys for myself. This one focuses in futility and seems to ramble on, its course uninterrupted. I must become a path finder, a better map maker for myself.)

Third semester renewed the struggle to study. Berrigan's lack of interest in school and the limbo of her relationship with Linda both spelled the approach of a definite change. She was contemplating abandonment: of Bingham College, Linda Framer, and her own hope in trusting women. The idea only catalyzed when Linda revived her affair with Gene.

Linda had started an unexpected change pattern of her own. She was never in the dorm room anymore, and she seldom called. The desertion almost immediately followed her return from Hartford when Berrigan accompanied her. Even Linda's mail and phone messages lay unanswered for days at a time. The weekly checks her parents sent were not picked up. Everything with Linda was sudden, impulsive: the war on Berrigan; her unexpected defense of Berrigan to Cobb, risking her own frat-set position; the grandstand kiss on the roof of Jensen Hall; the trip to visit her parents in Hartford; woodnymphs in a cornfield, lovers in stolen hours in Room 620. And now, just as easily as she had initiated these actions, came her abject dismissal of them all. It had only been another fad for her. "Out of the frat set, into the queer vat," Berrigan could hear Linda joking.

As Berrigan thought over all that had happened since she met Linda and they became lovers, and all that had *not* happened, her restless nervousness heightened. They had never really communicated, only exchanged words. Linda's concentration on self did not allow for their development of any common ground. Her aspirations would never change; she had come this far Hartford born-and-bred and she would end up "proper," traditional, fulfilled by some man. A confrontation seemed imminent. For Berrigan there was no more extension of her values to give, and she knew she must come to terms with Linda and with herself. The right to expectations had ended.

Sitting in BJ's, on the off chance of finding Linda there, Berrigan played out their closing scene like the denouement of a Bogart picture.

(So long, Schweethaht. It was nice knowin' ya. I'll never forget you, kid. Maybe I'll see you again sometime. In Casa Blanca.)

If their relationship had not really been romantic, at least their parting could be. Lost in the vision of herself in a slouch hat, leaving Linda amid pouring rain, Berrigan was jolted from her daydream by the voice of a stranger.

"Pardon me, but aren't you Linda Framer's roommate?"

Berrigan looked into the quizzical face of the Framers' neighbor, the rightly-bred daughter of the Mayor of Hartford.

"My name is Evelyn Walker. My family are good friends with Linda's parents. They're worried because she hasn't returned any of the messages or phone calls from them. Do you know how I can get hold of her? I mean, is she all right so I can just call to let them know? I told them I'd find out when I got down here; I've just transferred in as an Accounting major."

Over BJ's pizza supreme, Berrigan assured Evelyn that Linda was not only all right, but apparently so preoccupied with something or someone on campus that hardly anyone could locate her. *"I've only been able to catch glimpses of her when she drops by for a change of clothes. The last I heard, she was concentrating on a guy named Gene Rally. But with Linda, there's some new interest every other day so it's hard to say if she's still with him. But you can assure her parents that her campus involvements are acceptable and her attentions properly directed. Just don't mention that she's flunking out."*

Evelyn proved more perceptive than Berrigan judged. "And shall I tell them Linda's friend Berrigan sends her best wishes?"

One of those very special deep smiles slipped out across Berrigan's face. There had been few in the last months.

"Someday you'll be famous for that smile."

"And you for your instant insights, no doubt! Pass the pizza!"

The news that Berrigan was being repeatedly seen in the

21

company of the Hartford Mayor's daughter traveled quickly across the small BC campus. They became a hot item, although many speculators, allowing for Evelyn's status, placed her above suspicion. She was most likely exercising some samaritanism by befriending the campus lesbian. Wherever Linda had been sequestered, she soon came out of hiding to reclaim her "territory." But the dramatics did not impress Berrigan. When Linda returned to Room 620, she found it half vacant. Campus skeptics were confounded: Berrigan and Evelyn Walker had moved in together.

CHAPTER 3

"Linda Framer's parents will crap, Evelyn, absolutely keel over!"

"Good. We'll give them a new 'Family Forum' topic. Maybe we'll even end up in their Christmas letter. I can see our blurb now: 'Dear Friends: we've spent the better part of this year incredulous and disgusted over the unexpected relationship between Evelyn Walker and a very questionable Bingham woman, Berrigan. And to think Linda and Evelyn used to be in the same swim club! Whatever happens to all the good girls these days?' "

"You were really in the same swim club?"

"Are you kidding? Linda and I were the water wizards of Hartford's Country Club! We got breasts before anyone else did and so we were better floaters. Being an aqua-deb has made me what I am today!"

"What you are today is in hot water. You've been branded a dyke sympathizer, which is much worse than being an Indian giver or even a commie pinko. Evelyn, aren't you worried about this affecting your heavy dater reputation?"

"I'm more worried about how it affects my allowance from my father, his honor The Mayor!"

Despite the rumors and gossip and questions, Berrigan and Evelyn had made an instant connection and were determined to develop a friendship. They became kite flying beer buddies, sharing 3-dip sundaes and attempted tune-ups on Evelyn's old VW. Evelyn loved any hint of adventure; Berrigan was drawn into her risk-taking schemes. The women offered each other an unassuming support and insulation from collegiate trivia. At once friends and comrades in no cause larger than good times, they were not afraid to touch but dispensed with further analysis of it.

At times, though, the world seemed like a jungle to Berrigan: memories of Linda rushing into her consciousness were like a haze of confusion. She felt as if she was standing still, stalling, avoiding any move towards taking up the Amazon labyris to start carving a new way of living.

Evelyn had her own struggle. Though she often disdained her privileged upbringing, she was not yet ready to jettison the financial freedom of her father's status and generous allowance. She tried to view her own mixed feelings nonchalantly.

23

"The constraints of status can have drawbacks," she told Berrigan. "After all, it is a well known fact that Hartford debutantes do not menstruate. The thought of two pounds of Kotex underneath all those pampered fashions is anathema!"

Like leaning walls of flesh, Berrigan and Evelyn came to call upon one another when days sagged or horizons faded, leaving them jiggling, nervous at land's end with no boundaries in sight.

Evelyn was an avid reader, occasionally dabbling in analytical essay writing or literary review. She encouraged Berrigan to write as well, in forms less restricted than Intro. to English assignments. So Berrigan began a journal — of poems, thoughts, hypothetical questions and theories which she wrote down as they occurred, stream of consciousness. She was known to run nude and dripping from the shower, screaming a notable line that had come to her, and recording it immediately in her journal.

The support of Evelyn's friendship helped Berrigan complete her first year at BC, enduring bothersome school time so that she could break out of her college boredom for escapades with Evelyn. Their most noted coup involved the BC student newspaper, The Bulletin, for which Evelyn wrote an occasional "society" column. Circulation was down at the Bulletin, and the editor wanted a scoop that would guarantee renewed interest in the paper.

Sensing an adventure about to unfold, Evelyn approached him with the idea that boosted Cosmo ratings: a nude beefcake centerfold. At first the editor balked, but Evelyn bolstered him with a rousing pep talk on assertive journalistic freedom and the necessity of appealing to public interest. "What sells better than sex?" she concluded. The editor finally agreed to give her a shot at getting a centerfold photo. The only condition was that she was not to get caught!

Conferring with Berrigan on a plan of action, Evelyn bribed a janitor into giving them a peek at the football locker room. To their delight, they found that vents to a storage space underneath the floor afforded a view of the entire locker room. If they could sneak into the storage area before a game, there was just enough of an opening created by the vents for the camera.

The ultimate risk came in getting into the storage space before the arrival of the players. This could be achieved if they were willing to endure two or three hours in the cramped quarters so that they would be in place earlier than the players filing in for pre-game preparations.

Resolving to sweat out this wait, the two women stocked up on munchies, an ice water jug, loaded two cameras, and hunkered down into the storage area directly in front of the vents.

Luckily, the shutters of Evelyn's cameras were drowned out by the tumult of the footballers preparing for their contest: noisy jock braggadocio, locker doors clanging, reels of athletic tape being unraveled and torn in half. For two hours, they briskly focused and

24

fired off three rolls of film, hoping for that one clear frame of the macho au naturel. The team huddled together for their rousing pep cheer and clattered out onto the field on eager cleats.

Berrigan and Evelyn emerged from their clandestine fox hole and raced to the Bulletin darkroom. They labored furiously to develop the film. To their complete dismay, they found they had succeeded in snapping 60 pictures of wet feet, crumpled towels, and the occasional bare ass, all through a thick cloud of talcum powder.

* * * * * *

Evelyn's saving grace was that she had not been overdosed with the feminine ethic. She did not feel required, even by her Hartford status, to keep constant company with men nor to prefer their company to her time with women friends. She did realize, however, that it was easier in Bingham to choose her companions, whereas in Hartford her father frequently enjoined her in dates with men she found completely unattractive. She openly enjoyed a certain control over men in the dating situation, but tired rapidly of the games involved. Though Evelyn was aware of the power her appearance could have with men, Berrigan observed that she kept all her real poses of beauty to share with women.

Their few friends could not simply categorize nor finalize conclusions about the relations between Berrigan and Evelyn, and most eventually dispensed with trying to do so. Evelyn was good counsel and company, always willing to drop everything and fly after good times on the spur of the moment. Berrigan was too pleasant to leave anyone critical of her, though she seemed very serious and saw almost everything on the same level of intense importance. Their two separate army cots in the same room did not afford easy interpretation, but most of their friends saw that Berrigan and Evelyn held something special for each other, a unique love affair with a new concept of consummation.

Perhaps that link people tried to recognize about Evelyn and Berrigan was not a simple one to spot. Their soul touching came in their mutual willingness to play, without being embarrassed if judged immature. They would gallop to plunky tinny tunes on two frowning carousel horses (used to smaller riders). Their laughter spread over the carnival music as they let out the free children still inside them, kept so often in cobwebbed corners of the adult soul.

Walking out on a sandbar in the middle of the Dovey River, which ran through Bingham Square, Berrigan and her friend saved a crab turned on its back.

Over the bridge, they touched hands. Berrigan kicked a can and poked in the weeds with a stick. Evelyn looked into the water and followed her reflection in widening ripples. The two of them yelled into a cement bunker trying to make echoes, had contests with skipping stones, blew the tops off a thousand dandelions.

25

Then, pulling and pushing each other up the bank of the Dovey, they appeared on the street home with tufts of the dandelion still in their hair, the joy of friendship and children tired from good play slick upon their spirits. Here then was the truth of their bonding: they had not grown afraid of the children in them that loved uninhibited frolic, bare feet in spring grass, mud squeezed up between the toes.

Meanwhile, the emergence of Berrigan's consciousness raced on, and feminist poems were beginning to appear in her journal more and more, styled often without elegance, briskly eager. She would read a book on detailed theory, and respond in poetry, bursting upon the pages as she let go, one by one, of the carefully constructed barricades her past had built in her. She even found the beginnings of some explicitly lesbian love poetry within herself.

Sometimes she wrote in prose:

"What will I lose in exchanging men for the women who can fill me full of songs of myself? This Berrigan-womb was chosen in karmic rites to bear sapphic poems, not doe-eyed babes. One day we will all be sisters in the dance of love, breaking out of the winter of man-touch, away from all the Ray Purty's, away from these lassoes of historic possession."

Eager for both of them to keep reading and writing, yet stagnated by the strident academic approach to literature offered at BC, Evelyn initiated their participation in a newly forming independent writing group. Calling themselves "The Passionate Few," the group of four men and three women were all interested in experimenting with writing skills. Berrigan was electrified by the enthusiasm of the group. At last she seemed to find a sanctuary for her expression.

Within the group, styles and themes varied but all agreed on the necessity of patience, trial and error, constant writing. Evelyn's themes tended toward the intellectual, Berrigan's to the emotional. They were dubbed by their fellow writers, "Dr. Head and Dr. Heart."

After meeting several months, The Passionate Few decided to compile a booklet of the best selections each writer had done and distribute this through BC. Berrigan chose a long poem she had composed about the ancient feminaries: Aeolians, Amazons, those lost links to her own feminist strength. Evelyn submitted a literary review of *The Shrews*, a collection of Russian poets, women little known or read in this country.

The booklet was critically acclaimed by the artistic dissidents in Bingham, marginally noted by most of BC's students, and trounced by the literary "establishment" at the college. This reception spurred Berrigan and Evelyn in opposite directions. Berrigan decided to quit school and stop wasting her time within confines of academic perspective. She would attempt to freelance her poetry to feminist newspapers and magazines. On the other hand, Evelyn vowed to intensify her studies towards getting a CPA so she could start her own business to snafu the "system."

"I'll build up a savings reserve and fund artists who are strangled by pseudo-liberals patronizing them or radical conservatives still crying 'heresy!' Of course, you'll be in charge of that fund, Berrigan, and you can write all my advertising."

"Oh sure! I can see that now. 'Come one, come all ye oppressed, to find salvation in the accounting wizardry of Evelyn Walker, CPA! Women, blacks, elderly, handicapped, dykes: Welcome!' His honor the mayor wouldn't even think of seeking re-election if you hang out a shingle like that!"

"You mean strong, outspoken independent daughters are not viewed as political assets?"

"Only if they have no personal politics!"

* * * * * *

Berrigan located the name and address of a women's bookstore in New York and from their mailing list obtained copies of several popular political newspapers. These she shared with Evelyn, whose natural intellectual curiosity led her to devour this new kind of writing perspective. They marveled at the many issues-within-issues they had never considered, and the sophistication obvious in some of the more "slick" literary magazines. Their favorite section of these publications were the "coming out" stories. All manner of techniques were exhibited in these, from maudlin melodrama to terse accounts of the "pain and searching" to candid remembering of the bliss of first love.

In reading a particularly graphic coming out story, Evelyn admitted to having been naive about some lesbian sexual practices which were detailed in the story. Berrigan chided her, disbelieving her lack of knowledge.

"I never claimed I was an expert on lesbians, you know. To know one is not to know all things on the subject!"

"As a matter of fact, you've never told me how you learned about lesbians, Evelyn. So fess up! Was it hinted at darkly in a psychology class? Or giggled about in P.E.?"

"No, nothing as perverse as that. Frankly, as I recall, I had a girlfriend when I was eight and we loved to spend the night together. We'd hug and kiss and spend hours in the shower trying to snap each other with a wet towel. That's probably the only unconditional trust I've ever felt with another person and I didn't even know it! It's too bad I was not the genius at eight that I am today! Probably if someone had wanted to, they could have misconstrued our closeness and made us feel guilty. But as I look back on it, feeling guilty would only have been a way of keeping us apart. A male plot, no doubt! It seems perfectly natural to me for girls that age to love each other exclusively. Boys at eight are such clumsy dullards! I wouldn't call that incident lesbian, but since I've been reading with you about women and bonding, I think differently about it, more positively. I'm glad I had that experience.

"But the first time I actually found out about the *word* lesbian was during my sophomore year of high school, when I joined a drama group. Pep club and cheerleader weren't for me. Too much sweating for a debutante, after all! Debate was a prestige ultimate, but I couldn't make that grade so I went into duet acting and giving readings. Now you know how kids can be in high school, even the private school I attended, supposedly the 'creme de la creme!' But the same ole bullshit peer pressure, jealousy, and petty wrangling goes on.

"I had a personal battle going with two junior debaters: Christie Fargess and Anatole Benchley. Christie touted her good looks to everyone and Anatole thought she was hot shit because of her name. They were good debaters, but they were such snips!

"Anyway, they used to always tease me because I thought I was hot shit over my breasts and swim club but I hadn't made it into debate. We were all talented but obnoxious as hell in our struggles with pubescent urgencies, zits, and prestige.

"Talk about competitive! Drama and debate was all part of the same class and sabotage ran high: we stole each other's notebooks right before a test, and Anatole even went so far as to put a sack of sour garbage in my locker. I'm sure she paid a freshman to do that — she herself would never handle garbage, not even for revenge on me! But our favorite trick was to try and run each other's hose. One time, Christie and Anatole grabbed me just as class dismissed and the hall filled with students. In the rush, no one could see them give my garter belt two quick scissor snips. In the aftermath, I was standing red-faced in the hallowed hallway of the Hartford Academy for Girls with my hose coiled merciless around my ankles."

Berrigan, laughing, commented, *"God, I bet you were embarrassed!"* Evelyn nodded.

"Luckily I was not the only underdog in the drama class. I had a friend in misery, Holly Marple, daughter of a Westinghouse VP. She was more experienced than I in the matter of boys, and so when we weren't busy preguessing the next act of sabotage Anatole and Christie might try, we were discussing sex and how far to go. Holly was on the verge of going all the way, despite my counsel that she hold off.

"After an evening of insistent jostling in the back seat of a car with a guy she thought she loved, Holly came to me upset and weepy. We stepped into a stairwell so our conversation would not be intercepted by any of our teachers, those ardent guardians of our proper growth and development.

"Who should appear to witness this exchange of compassion but our arch-rivals, Christie and Anatole. Sighting us in our cubbyhole of distress, they chanted, 'Thesbians, thesbians, you two are thesbians!' A tearful Holly grew indignant and challenged them.

" 'You don't even know what a thesbian is, so go blow off!' "

"Anatole snorted. 'You're the ignorant ones! If you knew what thesbians were, you wouldn't be hugging in the stairwell!'

" 'We weren't hugging!' I stormed. 'Holly's upset about . . .' whereupon Holly's hand clapped securely over my mouth.

" 'Thesbians had to live on an island away from everyone else because they were so dirty,' Christie told us in a 'nyeah-nyeah' voice. 'Alls they did was wear gowns and suck grapes. That's why people called them fruits! They just laid around kissing each other and playing on lutes!'

" 'Yeah, lutes!' Anatole agreed. 'They were burned in England for being nasty and kidnapping children and robbing old ladies! In mythology, Zeus found out his own daughter was a thesbian and turned her face into a bunch of snakes!'

"I thought then that Holly might forget all her well-coaxed manners and jump on Anatole and pull her hair. But the Juniors figured they'd made their point and ran up the stairs, echoing back at us, 'Thesbians, thesbians, faces full of snakes!'

"I asked Holly if there was such a thing as a thesbian but she wasn't sure. 'But I don't think you better ask anyone either.' Knowing me, I wasn't about to ponder long. Just as Holly ignored my advice not to surge into womanhood too soon, I ignored her advice to keep the taunt of thesbian to myself.

"I went to the source of answers for all my questions, my mother. She was good about not making me feel stupid, even though I'm sure I jolted her by discussing such things as farting in the movies. I wasn't sure she was ready to decipher thesbians to me but I had to know. I knew I could count on that secret liberal part of her to enlighten me. Underneath that well manicured, golf-at-nine/bridge-at-four society matron burned a spark of free thought! This aspect of herself she shared with me only when we were completely alone and my father was nowhere in sight. In such rare moments, I found out wonderful things about her: she believed in reincarnation, loved unicorns, and avidly read history books about frontier settlement. 'How do you think our French Regency furniture would have looked in a sod house?' she once joked with me.

"When I related my encounter with Christie and Anatole to her, omitting of course the true nature of Holly's dismay, Mother patted me with her cool hand.

" 'Evelyn, girls will probably be jealous of you all your life. So you must expect that they may be cruel. Envy has a way of making one short-sighted. A thespian is a person who acts, like you, in drama. A lesbian is a woman who loves other women. Anatole and Christie have managed ably to confuse the two,' she told me.

"My mother's cool hand upon me was benediction for complete resolve and safety. I asked her if lesbians were dirty and nasty lute

29

players and if it was true they were burned. Were they still burned? I'll never forget what my mother told me.

" 'Some people view anything different as evil and nasty,' she told me. 'I don't know about the lutes; they are a unique instrument with a beautiful sound. Lesbians probably were burned as witches and I guess they still are, in a way. You know, burned by insults and judgements.

" 'Sarah Bernhardt was a *thespian,* very famous and successful. She had great strength as a dramatic artist, but was not made masculine by a strenuous career. I would be proud of you if you were like her. But I'm proud of you anyway."

Evelyn sat quietly for a moment when she finished her story, savoring the memory of the conversation with her mother. Berrigan respected her silence, saying nothing to interrupt her thoughts. Finally Evelyn said, "So that's my story on lesbian thespians."

"There's a nice story there about mothers and daughters, too."

"Uh huh. Come on. Let's go fly a kite!"

* * * * * *

Though the dream of a business together working for the good of the mistreated masses was fun to envision, Berrigan knew her life with Evelyn offered a cloistered safety. She was becoming a lame cat in her dependence on their friendship.

Zany adventures and kite flying with Evelyn were no solution to dealing with the difficult questions Berrigan knew she had to answer for her own development. Her freelance correspondence with feminist publications was one step in the right direction, bolstered by her reading of feminist theory and herstory, the documents of revolution.

While Evelyn's support and consideration had enhanced an atmosphere for this feminist study, she could not be Berrigan's translator for learning the new language of freedom, that spoken by a new generation of Amazons. And so Berrigan knew the time was nearing to leave the shore and risk a dive into the waves.

CHAPTER 4

Berrigan quickly learned that trying to pay the rent by writing articles and poetry for feminist publications could be difficult. She had some initial success with a short story and several poems. But between the limited budgets of most feminist papers and Berrigan's own need to develop her writing abilities further, she knew she was not yet ready to "live by her art." Even though Evelyn was willing to contribute extra money for their expenses, Berrigan wanted to be fair to her friend and be realistic with herself.

Replying to an ad for a part-time grocery clerk, Berrigan met the owner of Amil's market. The store — small, old fashioned, and located in a Jewish neighborhood — served as much as a social club as it did for the dispensing of aspirin and corned beef. Amil Kostowentz liked to pretend he was grumpy. At first he refused to consider Berrigan for the job.

"You from the college, huh? Got lotsa big ideas about how to run the world, huh?"

Berrigan explained she wasn't in school any more. Amil remained unsympathetic.

"It wouldn't work out. You got no experience."

Berrigan grew impatient. *"What's with you, anyway? I need this job, I can run the register, and I'm available. Or don't you want to hire a woman?"*

"What? I ain't prejudas! But let me tell you," Amil said, waving a finger fat as a sausage at her. "After dark around here ain't no picnic! I been robbed before!" He squinted at Berrigan, who, unmoved by his warning ploy, squinted back.

"You protect me if someone comes in here with a gun?" Amil asked her, softening, teasing. "You can lift those stock boxes, yes?"

"Yes," she answered, unafraid, testing him back.

"Well then, okay! But no flirting on the job, you hear?" he barked, again waggling the sausage finger.

"Of course not!" she grinned.

The new job at the market and time for Berrigan's writing seemed compatible. Evelyn was pleased with Berrigan's show of initiative, although they had less time together. Her own pace in school had picked up and she needed more hours for study.

As part of her new outlook, Berrigan was giving some thought to attending a meeting of Bingham's chapter of NAW — National

31

Alliance of Women. Although she was not inclined towards groups, she felt a growing need to be with activist women and NAW provided that opportunity in Bingham. As she was searching the Bingham Spoiler, the town newspaper, for an announcement of community meetings, Amil questioned her, in his teasing way.

"Loafing on the job again! I ain't never hired a woman before and this is why! Always got an eye on a sale! What you lookin' to buy this time? China or silver?"

"Neither. I'm looking for a NAW meeting schedule."

"NAW? What's that?"

"The Bingham Women's Group: National Alliance of Women."

"Oh sure, sure: Women's Lib! Phooey, I don't want no part of that! We got one of them comes in here always screamin' and yellin' about prices. Women should be ladies, not crazies. Women should be . . ." Amil was stopped by the look on Berrigan's face. His teasing was friendly but also challenging, and with Berrigan, he quickly learned there were times when the challenge went too far.

"Well, you'll see what I mean," he concluded and went to the produce counter to polish apples.

Several days later, as Berrigan was taking inventory at the back of the store, she overheard Amil and a woman arguing in loud voices. .

"I can't believe this hamburger! Two months ago that price would have bought steak! And what about this fruit? What's it made of, gold? I've got a baby at home to feed! I can hardly afford milk for him with these black market prices! I'm turning you in to the Better Business people. There oughta be a law!"

"If you don't want kosher, go somewhere else!"

Amil came flying back to the stock room, his apron tails fluttering, his cheeks flushed. He grabbed at a box in the corner, pulling from it a sequestered whiskey bottle. After a drink of the whiskey, he sputtered some very rude Yiddish, flapping at Berrigan to go take over the register.

As Berrigan approached the checkout counter, she saw two of Amil's regular customers clucking and nodding excitedly, watching another woman angrily placing her groceries in a sack.

"Can I help you?" Berrigan offered.

"I don't need *any* help or sympathy or . . ."

The woman stopped when she turned around to face Berrigan. Her shoulders sank a little then. She looked at the other women in the store who were staring at her.

"I'm sorry, really. I just can't handle the frustration sometimes. The prices aren't Amil's fault. But I'm trying to keep myself and a 10-month old kid fed. It's murder! No one knows what it is to be a woman alone with a child."

And with that, she marched out, jockeying her sacks, powering down the street on raw pride.

After the woman was gone, Berrigan went to find Amil. He

32

was slumped against some fruit crates, his whiskey bottle nearly empty.

"*Are you all right, Amil?*"

"What can I do? I'm sorry about her kid. But we all gotta live; *me* too!"

"*Who is she? Do you know her?*"

"She's in with that NAW group, I think. Her name is Cox, Syru Cox. She's in the paper sometimes."

Amil finished the whiskey with a resonant belch. He and Berrigan were holding each others eyes for a moment.

"Crazies, these women's libbers," he said in a voice soft with liquor and pity, "all crazies."

The roar and fury of Syru Cox didn't reoccur at Amil's market. Berrigan didn't see her again until she wandered into Bingham Square on a late October evening. The street lights were lit and gleaming, a historic touch Bingham was proud of. A small crowd had assembled around eight or nine women standing on a makeshift stage. Other women were distributing flyers to the people in the crowd.

Edging up closer to the audience, Berrigan heard a tall woman with red hair who was wrapped in a thick shawl.

"Ladies and gentlemen! Bingham is behind! Progressive legislation is passing our city and state by! The ERA is up for state vote and we must go to the polls! Women are victims of sex discrimination: evidence exists within Bingham businesses and employment opportunities. Only with the ERA can we hope to make a dent in this pervasive sexism!"

Next a heavy woman in knickers and striped knee socks took over.

"Our city government is male-dominated. Why haven't we had a woman as mayor or council member? Why do our female teachers get paid less than male teachers for equal work loads? Why do Bingham banks consider women who are heads of households *greater* risks for loans than men of the same status? Most Bingham businesses do not provide for pregnancy leave with pay, or childcare expenses. Without the ERA, none of this will change."

And then Syru Cox spoke. She was hardly an Amazon in stature. Perhaps raising her voice that day at Amil's had made her seem giant and armor-plated. Energy emanated from her as she harangued her listeners in the Square only slightly more diplomatically that she had the shoppers at Amil's.

"Alice Paul preached this gospel over 50 years ago and I say it's high time we started listening! We can't afford to let the ERA be defeated. We all have an interest here. Perhaps many of you are satisfied, especially those of you who are housewives. That's fine, because this legislation will *not* force you to change your life. But it will provide you with options if *you* decide to change your life.

"Ask yourself if your daughters will be satisfied with the life

33

you lead when they come of age. How will you answer when they ask, 'Did you vote for my equality?' The world is changing and Bingham cannot ignore progress. We cannot stay enmired in an outdated value system that only respects women in traditional roles. It's time to stop corsetting strong intelligent independent women. We can only gain by guaranteeing all persons their individual freedom. NAW works for women and we believe the ERA will benefit all women, in this state and in the nation. Call your senators tomorrow! Tell them to vote *YES* for the ERA! You owe it to the future; it's a sound investment. Women are this country's most valuable natural resource."

Berrigan applauded, almost alone in her approval of the speech. The crowd began to disperse as the evening chill deepened. "Vote for the ERA! Give your sister her freedom!" Syru told women in the crowd as they passed her and she pressed a NAW leaflet upon them. As Berrigan took the leaflet, Syru brightened, recognizing her.

"You're from Amil's, right?"

"Yes."

"Glad to see you out here. But why haven't you been to any of our meetings before? We desperately need new input."

"A few more warm bodies wouldn't hurt either."

"Yeah, I know."

Syru looked at the other NAW women who were packing up the stage.

"They're dedicated, though. Most of them are only recently declared feminists, still busy defining and educating each other. What we need is some radical spirit! For awhile, I expect we'll be scapegoats around here for a lot of anti-woman flack. We're only a local branch of the national group. But once we get our womanpower unified and launched, people better stand back in Bingham!"

Syru's enthusiasm was infectious, positive feminist optimism. Berrigan wanted to hear more, yet her fear of imposing made her shy.

"Where's your baby?"

"At home. Which reminds me! My sitter is due at class at nine, and I'm late already."

"Can I help you carry this stuff?"

"Sure, and the company back to the house in the dark will be appreciated."

The NAW women made sketchy plans for a rap-session later in the week.

"Syru, do you think anyone was listening?"

"Sure they were! But did they *hear* what we said? It's hard to know."

One of the women told Syru, "I think you went a little heavy on the 'outdated value system' bit."

34

"Don't be so defensive! We can't talk pap on this or **pretend it** isn't important or ignore that we're oppressed. Just keep the faith! We've got to bombard them with the truth until they realize what we're saying."

"See you next week, Warrior!"

"Go with Diana!"

"Long live womanpower!"

Their laughter as they left jingled in the dark, leaving the street lamps lonely, empty globes full of nervous flickers. Berrigan and Syru trudged through troughs of leaves, their travel crunching hollow against the night. Six blocks from the square, they stopped at a sagging brownstone.

"Here it is: Syru's Hallowed Haven. Waifs and derelicts, behold!"

They climbed chipped cement stairs up to a musty second level. "Open sesame, Myrna!" The door drew back and the chain disengaged.

"Wonderwoman returns as Monster Mother, I see," Myrna, the sitter, chided. "He's asleep. He's so good when you're gone, Syru. What does that tell you?"

"Only that he inherited my charm and sense of good timing. Here's two bucks. Now go! It's past nine. And thanks, Myrna, you're a true sister. I'll call ya soon."

Myrna considered the two dollar bills. "Don't call me, Syru. I'll call you. Childcare on a *charity* basis is not what I call a growing enterprise!" Then she zoomed down the stairs, books in hand, scarves flailing, waving goodbye back to Syru standing in the doorway.

"Myrna's studying to paint nude self portraits," Syru told Berrigan. "You wouldn't believe the set of mirrors she's got!"

Berrigan set down the box of leaflets she was carrying.

"Take your coat off. I'll just go check the baby."

When Syru left, Berrigan surveyed the well-lived-in clutter of the apartment. The room smelled of toast and rusty water pipes; piles of paper lay in chaotic disarray. Books spilled out of a shelf in one corner. Berrigan walked to the shelf to look at the titles. *"Who are you, Syru Cox?"* she pondered at the back of her brain.

"The kid is okay. Sleeping belly up with no thought to the revolution," Syru said returning. Seeing Berrigan at the bookcase, she offered, "If you see anything you want to borrow, go ahead."

"No thanks. I've read most of these."

"What did you think of the rally?"

"I was surprised. I've never seen any women taking their politics to the streets before."

"Well, I guess that's sorta what we were doing, but a very mild version of what I've seen in New York and on the coast. When *those* women go out in the streets, people stop in their tracks and get liberated! Instant consciousness!"

"I'd like to see that happen!"

"Where are you coming from anyway? Are you a feminist? Do you want to be? Are you just interested but inactive? What are you reading? What are you *doing*? Why aren't you in NAW?"

These questions Syru fired at Berrigan without giving her a chance to answer.

"The problem with the feminist movement has to do with women like you. Your heads are turned on but you don't do anything from that point. Token feminists! Closet woman-warriors! You read Susan B. Anthony and go 'wow!' and yet marchers pass your house while you stare at them from your window. Your feminist power is all there, burning right underneath the surface, but you balk at the heat. The NAW women in Bingham really need you. Womanpower is just a jive word right now, a catchy media filler. But womanpower has the potential to be the pulp of unequaled history. People can only ignore us so long. Even so, some of our worst enemies are other women, those afraid to trust."

Syru's last comment struck a soft spot with Berrigan.

"Just a minute! You don't know what I think. Women are not the enemy."

Syru ignored Berrigan and went on, pacing back and forth, almost talking to herself.

"We've got to do everything we can on the local level. Make connections, deal with our socialization. It's only a small start, but all these satellite groups, NAW and others, add up to a growing force of women who refuse to be beginners any longer. So why aren't you doing your part? Why aren't you in NAW?"

Berrigan was surprised to find herself not as a casual observer at a NAW meeting as she had planned, but jutting jaws with the leader of NAW, who was demanding a justification of her politics.

"Well?"

"I don't owe you any explanations. Why do you have to be so . . ."

"What?"

"Intimidating?"

Syru laughed and started for the kitchen. "You gonna stay and have some cocoa?" She grabbed a book from a table near her and tossed it to Berrigan. "Check this out: *Creative Revolution.* It's new. You'll like it."

* * * * * *

Syru Cox: volatile, officious, obsessed with revolution and conversion, an articulate warrior, the feminist without any hope for popular appeal. She told Berrigan she meant to intimidate — women, so that they would look at their own lives; men, because she hoped their anger would eventually consume them. What was not immediately apparent about Syru was that her fiery feminist energies were stoked with private bitterness, centering mostly on her life as a student and wife in the 60's. Behind her unyielding

36

rhetoric and show of strength, she had a soft spot: questions held without answers from a past not entirely resolved.

Syru had always believed she was ahead of her time, and in her college days, the climate had been perfect for her to experiment with many choices. She had lived for several years with a black man; they both seriously believed they could transcend the nuclear family to a divine understanding of man-woman control factors. They wanted to breed a super-race, make love and not war, conjure a peace-and-paradise world without end. Their schemes fouled when they found their friends stealing their dope, both parents pushing them guiltily towards the altar, and the spiritual appreciation of rhythm as lousy birth control. Immediacy was upon them: they could not live on welfare, Syru was bulging with the pregnancy of their prototype, and their highs had become too expensive, permanently grounded. So Syru and her lover married, exchanging their life in hippy haven for the boredom of normalcy in a fifth floor buffet apartment. Both worked at low-paying jobs they hated. His parents financed their furniture. The baby cried at night and their sex got lousy and all the ambiguities caught up with them. "We used to have such mellow times, baby. What happened?" he would say. Syru began to chain smoke.

They had been in love under different circumstances. They were not in love with a financed couch, as fast-food clerks washing diapers in the sink. He could not decide how to leave without feeling like a failure, so Syru packed her belongings, and deserted all demands except her own. She found friends in a house for single mothers, quickly wandering out of the collapsed home-and-hearth into the Amazon Dream.

In the beginning, allying with feminism was labeled radical, regardless of specific politics. Desperate for her own niche, Syru thrived in this subversive, outrageous, new movement of women doing, saying and being, claiming their freedom shamelessly. She found an entire battalian of instant comrades. But she left the feminist mainstream as it became *truly* radical, not because she reached a point of dissidence, but because the women she knew wanted her to commit too deeply to raising her consciousness, dealing with her past. She could be friendly but not intimate, close but not revealing. Marriage and childbirth had closed those doors in her and she adamantly refused any grand reopenings. Not even for sisterhood was that pain worth reliving.

Having made drastic changes in her life, becoming an avowed woman-lover, Syru was not open about this with her Bingham sisters. She felt compromised about trying to explain herself to them. It would make her vulnerable and distract from her leadership, which she had determined was needed by NAW.

"I am not conceited," she told Berrigan when she claimed to have the best understanding of how to achieve a revolution for women. "I just trust my own wisdom and instinct. After all, I *know*

37

I come from a superior race!"

But whatever else she denied about her past and her radicalism, Syru could not deny the reality of Ju-Ju, her mulatto son. He was beautiful, sweet-tempered, the color of cocoa, adored and adopted by everyone who saw him. Syru brought him to the NAW rap sessions where he delighted in the attention of the women who passed him maternally from lap to lap. Syru joked about it.

"Ju-Ju will have nuzzled more bosoms by the time he's three than most men do in a life-time!"

Syru's positive drive had taken the NAW group out of its infancy and into flight from the nest, into the wild blue yonder of reality. Despite a marked difference in feminist consciousness between Syru and most of the NAW women, they accepted her as their mentor and were fed by the intensity of her personal drive. At her suggestion and under her supervision, the NAW chapter began a Speakers Bureau to promote the ERA, in hopes of raising votes for the state's ratification of the amendment. Topics had branched out from the ERA to other women's issues as interest in the Speakers Bureau increased. Even though the men in Bingham government were barely warming, the women in the community were at least willing to hear what the NAW women had to say.

Within the group ran a spirit of hopeful eagerness and discovery: women exploring their feelings about themselves and about other women for the first time. Unable to ignore Syru's urgings, Berrigan became involved in the NAW process of learning and growing. After her first few "get acquainted" meetings, she was able to exchange with the other women support and challenge, so that all of them felt sprigs of new confidence, warmth, openness. Berrigan began trusting and revealing herself, further developing her abilities to relate one-to-one. The NAW rap sessions were somehow different from what she had seen in women's groups before and had discussed with Doris in therapy. The NAW women had pride in themselves and they believed they could find answers to the many difficult questions involved in changing their lives as independent women. They found that sorting through all the propaganda they had been taught was not easy, but they were determined not to become discouraged.

Sometimes the process broke down; Syru grew restless and impatient. She seemed to act as though she had to pay the price of moving forward at the expense of pulling her sisters along. When the NAW women bogged down, unable to see the limitations or prejudices influencing them on a certain issue, Syru was often petulant about sharing her knowledge with them, or admitting that she did not have the answers they needed. She was not allowed these lapses of patience without question; sporadic arguments did occur. But the women concluded that it was all right to agree to disagree. They encouraged Syru in a leadership position, even though she thought them too willing to compromise. "Revolution will not happen to the wishy-washy," she would pout.

Though her temperament was not always amenable, Syru Cox was a mover and the successful catalyst within Bingham's NAW chapter. She knew how to manipulate the public NAW wished to reach with its message, and had initiated programs on topics in Bingham previously unexamined.

As the national statistics on rape began rising, and with the incidence of several rapes on the BC campus, one of the sororities requested that NAW organize a rape prevention program for them. The audience would include the younger campus Gamma Phi members as well as the alumni chapter. Syru was delighted with the opportunity and rallied the NAW chapter energies. After group consultation, extensive phone calling, and rental of AV aides, the program was set up. It would be presented in two parts: first, defining rape as a crime of violence and discussing myths about rape. This would be presented by Delia Martin, a NAW member who was a psychiatric social worker. The second half of the program would feature a film of police and hospital procedures, along with simple self-defense training.

Syru opened the program with a straight-forward description of the most grisly aspect of rape: it can happen any time to any woman. She was more than matter of fact. She intended to shock. Delia Martin from the Bingham Mental Health Clinic followed with an in-depth evaluation of rapist psychology, adding to Syru's comments her own startling conclusions: all men are capable of rape and most consider it.

For a moment when Delia finished speaking, the women in the audience shifted in their chairs, shell-shocked into silence by the uncompromising facts presented. Then they burst into applause and the buzz of excited conversation.

After Ann Walters of the Bingham Police Department showed a film on police interrogation of a rape victim, she then demonstrated self-defense tips. Jean Marsh, a nurse practitioner, discussed hospital procedure for rape victims and a victim's medical rights. Finally, the program was opened for a question-and-answer period.

There was no timidity about the questions, which ranged from those that could be answered briefly and quickly, to those requiring more time and often Syru's suggestion of resource books for more complete answers. Responses to information in the program, especially Delia's part, were not hard to gauge. Most of the women hadn't realized the social implications of rape, and appreciated Delia's having defrocked the myths for them. There was some further debate from a few who weren't convinced on the violence-passion question, but Syru reiterated and expanded Delia's comments and soon even the few dissenters were nodding in agreement with her. She thrived on the give-and-take, glowing with energy when she was able to dispense at ease with queries.

In the next edition of the Bingham Spoiler, a woman reporting on the NAW program offered accolades, lauding the content, organization, and direct approach to the subject. The chapter women celebrated, sure this one small victory was only the beginning of many. They had been heard.

The women of Gamma Phi were not the only ones affected by the rape prevention program. It sparked a particularly vivid memory from Berrigan's past, a painful one but luckily the only one when the politics of sexism had been an imminent physical threat to her. She remembered her senior year in high school, and Robin Daltry III, the handsome young aide hired to help her father. He had the dashing aura of those heart-stealing men in dimestore romance novels. But his self-confidence was obnoxious, his cocksure charm irritating to Berrigan. Unlike her father, she was not impressed with Daltry's constant posing or his consuming ambition. He was convinced that his musk oil, styled bravado, and shyster smile would make him a VP in short order. Never mind that his business marksmanship was poor; at least he had the gift of "PR."

After several weeks of hearing the data on Robin Daltry III from her father, Berrigan was introduced to him at a company dinner. She was not convinced; behind his flattery and despite his impeccable pin-stripe suit, there lurked in Robin Daltry the odor of phoney baloney, something sneaky and dangerous. Berrigan was glad to be at a party with other people so she could keep her distance from him.

Berrigan was not blind to the matchmaking ideas forming in her father's mind. But before he had a chance to suggest anything directly, Daltry played his own hand. He was foolish, not knowing that Berrigan could spot warning markers and pirate ships a mile away.

Heeding her intuition about Daltry, Berrigan refused several offers to date him. She had talked to him by phone one evening when her parents went out to a movie; with his usual sense of opportunity paramount, Daltry came to the house, knowing Berrigan was alone there. Surprised that he showed up at the house after she'd refused yet another offer to go out with him, Berrigan remembered how he looked at the door: different somehow, almost as though a light had clicked on inside him. He was hyper, restless, his conversation no longer charming and urbane. She felt like a safe being cased for a robbery.

(You're not debauching my box, Robin Daltry!)

Daltry watched her, and looked out the window, listening to the cars passing in the street. "Berrigan, even in our few meetings, I've grown fond of you. Come over here on the couch and sit by me." He smiled at her, and patted the cushion next to him.

(Here's a cookie, here's some bait. Now drop those skirts, don't make me wait!) 40

"I'm really not in the mood to visit tonight, Robin. I thought I made that clear over the phone. I'm tired. Why don't we take a raincheck on conversation till another day when I feel up to par."

"Come here. I'll rub your shoulders. You'll feel better."

"I just want to go to bed. Would you mind?" Berrigan gestured toward the front door. Daltry ignored her implication that he should leave.

"Not if I can join you!"

He wasn't joking.

(You're an ice bastard, Robin Daltry, slick and treacherous.)

"I'm not in the mood for your persistence or your flippancy. Don't make me insist you leave. Why not be a good guy and volunteer?"

"I've never been a good exit man. It's not the kind of volunteer work I prefer. Now don't *you* make *me* insist on your participation."

(He's stalking me, mocking my defenses!)

"You're no prude, Berrigan. What are we waiting for? You think I believe all that stuff you have been giving me about *not* wanting to go out with me? Fat chance! All you chicks are alike. *No* always means *yes!* Mom and Dad will be home soon, so time's awasting."

And now Berrigan was able to see that the light in Robin Daltry was his excitement at the prospect of debauching her right under her father's nose.

"Do you really think that just because your sisters were social debs in Boston and because you ran for the touchdown that saved your conference championship, I have even the slightest interest in letting you roll me in my father's livingroom?"

"Quit stalling. Let's get down to it."

"Tell you what, Robin. Why don't you just tell my father you fucked me and skip the real thing. I'm not your type anyway. I'm not squirmy."

"Sorry babe. I've never been very good at make-believe. I've always enjoyed the real action: contact sports!"

Berrigan tried to pass him and go out of the room and towards the front door, but he caught her wrist and dragged her back towards the couch. She tripped him on the way and they fell down. In their grapple-fest, they jockeyed for advantage: Berrigan trying to get her hands free, Daltry trying to pin her. He was able to get his fly open but let go of one of Berrigan's hands to get at her clothing. With just that margin, she clubbed him in the temple with her fist, and then grabbed a heavy crystal penguin off a coffee-table which she slammed into his face on the bone above his eye. He relaxed just a moment as the blow stunned him and a gash flowing blood opened. But Berrigan could not twist over on her side enough to throw him off of her. They were an unfunny wrestling jumble of legs, arms, bobbling genitalia and bleeding brow, sounding in the grunts of frustrated stalemated foes and the whumps of Berrigan's fists on Daltry's back.

41

He pushed on her shoulders, locked his elbows and looked down on her, shaking his head till drops of blood spattered on her face.

"Why do you refuse me? Why are you fighting?"

"You never gave me a choice."

"You mean you really don't want to fuck with me?" He was incredulous. He was also getting fuzzy, his eye swelling shut. He rolled off Berrigan and tried to stand, slowly, clutching the bookcase. She jumped up, with the penguin still in her hand, and ran at him. He covered his face and yelled at her to stop. Startled, she lowered the penguin and banged clumsily into him. They were both panting, out of breath. Realizing Daltry was too woozy even to recover his phallic pride back to its Fruit of the Loom hideaway, Berrigan pushed away from him. The thought occurred to her to grab his penis and wrench it from side to side. But her rush of violence was gone. She could not touch him, even to wound him with his own weapon.

"Get out of here, you cheap bastard. Get out!"

In her memory of that night, Berrigan couldn't clearly recall Daltry leaving her father's house. She did remember that she made no attempt to hide the signs of their struggle, in particular the bloodied penguin. And she remembered realizing in her confusion and outrage that she could have struck Daltry again, possibly even killed him, bludgeoned him to death. Yet she had been as stunned as he when she hit him, even aghast at the resulting wound.

But now a particular picture from the whole incident came into focus in Berrigan's mind's eye: she had walked to the bathroom mirror to see a face, one she did not recognize as her own, its color washed out except for rusty dots of Daltry's blood. The collar of her shirt was crumpled, awry. Her hair ached at the back of her head where it had been pulled against the carpet during the struggle. As she looked at herself in the mirror, she had wondered who was responsible for the attack: Robin Daltry or herself.

Berrigan had not known when Robin Daltry attacked her that she had a right to fight to survive. The rape program convinced her of that; Syru's convictions bolstered her. She could finally erase a doubt that had lingered menacingly in her thoughts; she could feel comfortable that she had neither elicted nor yielded to Daltry's dementia.

After the rape program, Berrigan felt a complete commitment to NAW. Her friendship with Syru grew closer as well. Though they had much to offer each other, they did not always agree on all points. Such was the case within the chapter itself. The friction in the group came from an obvious difference in goals. Syru wanted to change the world and create an entirely new way of living, starting in Bingham. Most of the other women were only on the fringes of independence; they wanted reform, integration, equal pay for equal work. Though they listened attentively to Syru's endless monologues on the patriarchy, they did what they claimed most disgusted them about men: they tolerated her.

Disagreement was not always at the forefront of NAW, though, and Berrigan learned many things, was able to examine and analyze contemporary issues vital to women. She and Syru usually expressed their reactions to each meeting over cocoa at Syru's apartment.

"I got a lot out of the meeting tonight. Man-hating is a hard thing to talk about. You have to admit you're still letting men control you and not really giving your best to women."

"I think the best thing about the rap session was the general agreement that masculine qualities in women aren't bad, but that everyone wishes men would be a little more womanly: tender, patient, nurturing. Not always so aggressive."

"Wow, Margaret got really wound up there for awhile! I almost cracked up when she said we sounded like ball-busting war mongers!"

"I know. But I can't agree with her idea that we ought to spend a lot of time being fair and trying to educate men about feminism. Sometimes I think women are pathologically fair!"

"You have to give her credit though, for her persistence. Even after 16 years and two kids with a guy who dumped her, she still believes men can be saved, that we can work with them."

"She's persistent, all right; she's a genius at ignoring *my* point of view!"

"The warrior-orator foiled again!"

By the time she had become involved with NAW on a regular basis, Berrigan had lost her roommate. Evelyn had moved into the sorority house at the urging of her parents. It had not been an entirely painless process; they both cherished and missed the supportive companionship that had developed between them.

"But my father says the Walker college women have belonged to sororities for generations and I'll literally shake all the fruit from the family tree if I break with tradition," Evelyn bemoaned.

"Don't worry. You're going to look great in a Gamma Phi sweatshirt. All the other women will wish you'd never pledged!"

Though they worked shoulder-to-shoulder within the chapter, Berrigan still felt distant from Syru. Politically they were open and free. But on most other levels, their lifestyles were undefined to one another. Berrigan wished to know Syru better, but had so far been unable to make their time together move from the impersonal political level to the friend-to-friend level. She tried to get Syru to do things with her that did not always center on the polemics of sexism: seeing a movie, picnicking with Ju-Ju, bicycling. When Syru seemed skeptical of the latter, Berrigan used her own tactics on her. *"Revolutionaries can't afford to be weak in the knees!"*

Sometimes Berrigan's attempts succeeded and Syru could forget the wolf-whistles of the world and play as a woman of leisurely moments. She would soften at her edges, break into giggles, roll about in the grass with her son as though they were both nature babies. Then that unrelenting warrior would wake up again and Syru would return to her usual self: the impassioned feminist front-line spirit on permanent female soldiery alert.

Berrigan scanned the movie section of the Spoiler, suggesting to Syru that they retreat from the heat in her apartment to the alluring darkness of the theatre.

"Got the urge to act sleazy?" Syru teased. Berrigan raised her eyebrows in answer.

"Okay. What are our choices?"

" 'Beach Bunny Bingo,' plus extra added attraction, 'Frenzy on Blueberry Hill.' Also 'Klute,' or 'The Heart is a Lonely Hunter.' As usual, nothing that's been released in the last 5 years."

"What's showing at BC? You know, in the experimental film series?"

"Do I have to tell?"

"Uh huh."

" 'Emma Goldman: Portrait of a Revolutionary.' "

"Really?"

"That's not all. Also Bergman's 'Cries and Whispers.' "

"Well then! It's settled! You didn't really want to see that Beach Bunny Bingo thing, did you?"

"Sort of. At least that theatre believes in popcorn for their movies!"

"Don't despair! We'll make our own and take it with us!"

The movies acted as a transfusion for Syru; she was so revved as they walked home afterwards that she couldn't walk and talk fast enough. She was overwhelmed with a new burst of fervor. At one point underneath a stoplight, she grabbed Berrigan and began dancing them both round and round into the middle of the intersection.

"The woman-world is out there, just waiting for us to claim it, to raise the sunken temples of the Goddess, to proclaim our liberty! You're my only real comrade, Berrigan. You *know* what I'm saying when I tell the NAW women that *reform* is not enough! Let's be Emma Goldman born anew, together, now! Surging our furious feminist fists towards the sky in a roar of declaration! Freedom now! Women unbound!"

The light changed and cars began to honk at them so Berrigan lead Syru back to the safety of the curbside. Several teenage boys in a carload of their friends hollered, "Hey honey, howsabout a little? Wanna have a good time?"

"We need the revolution *now*," Syru said.

Back at Syru's apartment, they toasted the evening's end with their usual cocoa and then Berrigan got up to leave.

"It's pretty late so I better get home. I think I can catch a bus close by. I don't relish the thought of those guys in that car still being out and about."

"You ought to take a street fighting class so you'd lose some of that fear. At least you'd know more about your own reactions anyway."

"Is it always that easy, Syru? Take a class, read a book, everything just falls into place?"

Syru responded with a surprising and veiled offer. "The easiest answer is that you don't have to go home at all if you don't want to. You can stay here. Sleep anywhere you want."

For a moment there seemed to be a crack in the warrior's armor. But she was pretending not to notice. Syru left Berrigan standing in the livingroom holding her coat. She shut out the kitchen light and walked down the hall past Ju-Ju's room to her own bedroom. It was dark but the door was open. Berrigan was momentarily dumbfounded. How was this to be read? Reason was hiding, off-balance. Berrigan listened to the stillness of the rooms in the apartment, as if she hoped she could hear Syru waiting for her. All she heard was the clank of the water pipes on the first floor, and Ju-Ju's crib rattles when he turned in his sleep. Caution won out. She folded her coat for a pillow and curled up under the afghan on the couch.

At the next regular NAW meeting, the national convention in Washington was announced and the chapter began planning for their participation. Syru's mood was as ever: energetic, attentive, assertively rhetorical. She was busy organizing, suggesting steps to be taken, responding with encouragement to some ideas and with firm alternatives to others. Packets were distributed listing the convention agenda, scheduled workshops, registration forms, and other pertinent information. At once the women began to react.

"There are so many great workshops available! How will I be able to go to all the ones I want to? It's terrible to have to pick and choose which issues are more important," Marie commented.

Elaine agreed. "I wish I could be in two places at one time. I want to attend the Battered Women panel but also the Creative Divorce seminar, but they're on at the same time!"

"I think the diversity of topics is excellent," Syru offered. "Maybe we ought to divide the workshops up among those of us who are definitely going so that we bring back the most valuable information available for the advancement of the chapter."

"You don't mean assign panels, do you?" Alice was plaintive.

"Why not? I know we all want to use the convention for our own personal growth, but ultimately the chapter is most important."

"Come on, Syru!" Marie interrupted. "Can't we just go to the convention and have a good time and learn a lot about women's issues without the pressure of bringing back a 'chapter report'?"

"That's not my point, Marie." Syru could feel some resentment growing. "I'm just thinking about the benefit to the chapter. That's what's important *to me*."

Delia decided Syru needed some support. "I see your point, Syru. After all, we have to remember when the initial excitement of becoming feminists fades, there is no power unless we unite. The real opportunity for us in this convention has to do with what we can bring back to make our own chapter more effective, more in touch with women's issues."

Berrigan suggested a compromise. *"Why not select four or five key panels which one of each of us can cover and then leave the rest of the time open so that we can pick other panels of interest to us individually?"*

"Has anyone else noticed how many lesbian-feminist and radical-feminist panels there are?" Jan interjected, off the subject. "God, there's at least eight out of the total twenty-five. Does that mean there's going to be a lot of lesbians at the convention? In the same hotels with us?"

"Don't get nervous," Marie told her, patting her shoulder. "Remember what Syru keeps telling us: sisterhood can't be exclusive."

"Bullshit! I don't want a lesbian roommate!"

Delia could feel the increasing tension in the group. Syru was bristling. "Don't you think maybe you're reacting to stereotypes, Jan?" Delia asked. "Those lesbians have as much to learn from us as we do from them but we *both* ought to try."

"I'm with Jan," Alice chimed in. "I'm not so hot on all this lez jazz."

"Well, I think you're all missing the point," Elaine stated. "Learning about women's issues and making some friends with women from other parts of the country is what the convention means to me. If you can't deal with the radicals or the lesbians, go to another panel."

Everyone was seated in a circle for the meeting and Syru stood up, immediately setting herself off from everyone else. She walked around the chairs, looking at the other women.

"Wait just a minute here. What gives any of you the right to decide that lesbian-feminist panels are any less important than any other women's issue panel? I thought we had come farther than that. You all sound just like the men you live with. You ghettoize lesbians on the basis of your own ignorance. You don't know anything about it so the best thing to do is keep away from it. Oh and Elaine, your suggestion is terrific! Don't deal with it, don't even *try!* Ignore it even! With attitudes like these, you wonder why I go on tirades! You're so open-minded, I'm sure you'll learn a lot at the convention!"

"Not everyone feels the way Jan and Alice do, Syru. But you need to remember that the best way to deal with hesitance and ignorance is not to judge but to educate."

"Don't give me your last psychology lesson, Delia. We're all too damned polite and superficial as it is. All this pseudo-liberalism suffocates me! We could use a generous dose of self-criticism."

"*You're not exactly being generous yourself, Syru,*" Berrigan challenged. Syru was not ready for her comrade to question her. "What do you mean, Berrigan? You think it's ok for these women to go to that convention spouting anti-lesbian, anti-radical sentiments before they've met either at close range? You want the Bingham chapter to come across that way? The next thing you know they'll walk into the panel with black feminists and ask if it's true that all black men carry the Jolly Green Giant in their jeans!"

Jan was hurt and intimidated by Syru's remarks; she lashed out sarcastically. "Well now, Syru, I guess that's something *you* already know from experience."

Delia tried to defuse the anger. "I think there's enough cattyness and hate on the streets. We sure as hell don't need it in here too. Let's all cool off about this and give each other a chance. Let's break until next week."

There was no cheery parting with supportive slogans as the meeting ended; Syru as figurative leader had deserted her troops, gone into her own bitter shell. It was a tiny treachery, but just the kind of confrontation that kept the women at each other, untrusting and fearful. The conflict between Jan and Syru made everyone uncomfortable.

As the other women left, Berrigan confronted Syru more forcefully, charging her with giving lipservice to principles she didn't practice. She cited Syru with being judgmental, lacking empathy, begrudging about giving support for any compromise, no matter what the gain might be to the chapter. Syru was initially defensive, claiming she knew the politics of the NAW women better than Berrigan, who was "an uppity newcomer."

"You don't know their histories nor their vices like I do. So many of them come here beating their chests like the New Amazons and then go out dick-chasing like crazy."

Berrigan reiterated Delia's statement that consciousness raising is not an overnight process, one that doesn't benefit from pressure and belittling. Syru countered Berrigan's assessment of her behavior with the accusation that Berrigan's politics were no more to her than "something you do when you aren't punching out the price of peas." Berrigan questioned the effectiveness any feminist could expect, "*when she's so consumed by rhetoric that she overlooks her feelings. You talk about gut-level reactions all the time, but you don't ever share your own. And sharing is what sisterhood is about.*"

"Since you know so much about sisterhood and sharing, why aren't you out to the NAW women?"

The question stunned Berrigan, though she should have been used to Syru's directness. But she was learning how to use that same forthrightness back at Syru.

"*Seems like that's a question you ought to answer too.*"

47

The two women calculated each other, then Syru said, "I think Delia was right. We need to give each other a chance."

Once again Berrigan caught the glimmer of a crack in Syru's armor. She felt a slight loosening in Syru, a subtle shift towards those moments when she had been relaxed. Syru surprised her then by speaking about vulnerability. In just the little bit of herself that she let show, Berrigan felt how much pain from her past she still held.

Syru told Berrigan she could not allow herself to be vulnerable with the NAW women because their emotional turmoil as they evolved their answers drained her strength. What she did not say was that she was scared shitless they might still accept her even if they knew she too had struggled, out of a fifth-floor buffet and integrated domesticity. She could not admit even to Berrigan that she too had survived an evolution. It seemed she could not keep control if anyone thought they shared other common ground besides the grand cause of feminism. And for Syru, control was the only way to keep her pain and bitterness at bay.

For just a second as she spoke, Berrigan felt the shadow of doubt creeping into her voice.

"Sometimes I really feel like Jeckyl and Hyde. All the tuggings of my past battle all the urgencies of my present. I know I've got to stay on top of both of them to survive."

Berrigan hoped for a time when she could make Syru know that women can heal each other.

Berrigan conceded that she was not out to the NAW women because she not yet ready to deal with their reactions. *"I'm not ashamed, just unsure."* Syru, on the other hand, kept her sexual preference private only because, "It has served no political purpose so far to reveal it. All things in time." Berrigan was not completely convinced that Syru's motives were entirely political.

"So now you've taken me to task for my methods, are we going to the apartment? If so, just promise me one thing: this time you won't sleep on the couch."

Berrigan's Journal — Early November

We sat across from each other on Syru's rug, just looking at one another, untouching. It wasn't awkward or scarey. We were matching life vibrations, entering each other through our eyes. I felt all of Syru's great power pulling at my ineffectualities, tugging at me in little voices saying, "Amazon World, Mothers of Creation, Womanpower!" At first it seemed ridiculous and made me giddy. But then it settled into a rhythmic hum inside my head that matched my breathing, my heartbeat, like a love mantra. Then we sat closer, with our hands up before us, palms barely touching. I felt a symphony and the ocean pulsing in that small space between us.

I'm probably a romantic fool who will end up starving on my

48

idealism, but when I pick up Ju-Ju and he puts his head against me, how can I deny the hopefulness I feel? He makes me know that while I don't want to be a mother, I'm still a valid woman. For both of us, it's enough that I love his mother. Syru says he was more honest than she: he let me know he loved me right from the first.

* * * * * *

The love affair was not the spontaneous dive for unknown thrills Linda Framer had initiated with Berrigan. Berrigan's tryst with Syru evolved with friendship, at a gradual pace. There was no frantic pack-up by either of the women to establish a mutual household, though the excitement between them was undeniable. They shared great devotions: the feminist cause and individual freedom of expression. Inequalities were easier to bear with Syru's support; trust flourished through Ju-Ju in his infant's willingness to love.

Berrigan's Journal — November 17
Syru is so unpredictable. She makes me feel strong and shy at once. Sometimes I want to shake her for her impatience. Other times she turns into a new person: giving and loving. My ignorance of the movement of love is uncomfortable, but not unconquerable. I'm growing a little "patience plant" inside to help myself out. Body spaces overlap and we become the legs and arms and kissing mouths of proud and vital women lifting the magic of Sappho out of herstory, with our rising, falling, touching moans. The grandeur is perhaps only a personal magic for us to wonder at. But I know this: the experience of dying into sleep after tremendous climax and awakening against soft breasts was never destined solely to be a man's privilege. Sappho proved it on her island, and we re-prove it in our own sweet embrace. It escapes me now in any poetry, perhaps because the size of most verses could not contain it.

Berrigan's Journal — November 23 (attached note from Syru)
"Where have you been? I've endured a day without seeing you! In the Queendom of Songs, that is like a day of silence!
Yours, S. 'Sappho' "

Berrigan's Journal — November 27 (attached note to Syru from Berrigan)
"My house is howling for you as visitor! A bowl of jello in the fridge is forlorn, missing Ju-Ju's spoon. Could we meet here tonight? My intentions are not honorable!
Love, B. 'Diana' "

Berrigan's Journal — December 1
NAW meeting again tonight; everyone very chattery about the convention in January. Syru is elected as delegate spokeswo-

man for the Bingham chapter. Everyone wants to go; we set up a car-pool. Syru says we'll need plenty of "claquers:" women unafraid to vocalize their support and opposition on the convention floor. Ju-Ju makes a hit by dropping his diaper mid-meeting and parading around in proud nakedness among us. He is elected Phallic Mascot and considered to be the only true non-chauvinist male that any of us knows personally!

Berrigan's Journal — December 8
    Breakfast love-making, what a lark! What delicious rebellion! What sweet reward! Now a short parting while I help Evelyn study for her final exams.

Berrigan's Journal — December 10 (attached note from Syru)
    "The Christmas pressures begin upon us; already I dread our holiday separation. My mother is alone, and insistent that we come to see her in New York. Got several cards from old high school friends — it would be some deal to tell them about politics! They are all into nuclear familyism. If I had a warm back to sleep against tonight, I could forget myself for awhile. What comfort, a woman-lover! You are tender, needing no promise for sex.
                    S. 'Sappho' "

Berrigan's Journal — December 12 (attached note to Syru from Berrigan)
    "Cards and letters at Christmas time have always puzzled me. Silent ghosts from the past grow inebriated with seasonal Christian goodness, writing out their run-away emotions. Those who are lonely strike out with great cruelty (or jump from buildings). Threats or good wishes at Christmastime, warnings of caution delivered by the U.S. Mail — don't take them too seriously. Save that for my love.
                    B. Diana' "

Berrigan's Journal — December 20
    In the little out-of-the-way shops of Bingham, Syru and I found our Christmas exchange. For her, I bought a hanging pot candle with sand base and macrame beaded straps. In return, she gave me a silver candle-snuffer, with this message:
        "In the pot is set a candle, which like our love is burning strong. For you, a candle-snuffer, in case anything goes wrong. I trust you only to know when things are not right. So if I begin to waver, please put out the light."
    Syru's message was at once a vote of confidence and portent of an ending.

Berrigan's Journal — December 21
    Rapport with a child . . . . surely this is one of those incredible

favors the Goddess has dealt out sparingly. What an aching discovery to see all the wisdom in a baby I have not achieved as an adult. Ju-Ju gauges moods and spots deceit without effort or disdain. He receives everyone on equal basis, come-as-you-are. Until he is made uncomfortable or becomes afraid by something unnatural to him, anyone is welcome to his time and attention. He's just a baby, but he's made responsible because Syru is gone so often. He must know who to recognize as his protection when she leaves. I can tell a neglectful babysitter just by his behavior. Like all of us, he resents limbo. Syru loves him, but in a distracted and not intimate way. She isn't careless with him, only impersonal. He belongs to her, but sadly I think as a symbol rather than as a living person. I think perhaps he reminds her of that past she tries so hard to forget. And having a boy child frustrates her too. She worries how to raise him to be a "female man," a male who can truly love women. But it's not something anyone can change; it's a closed subject with Syru.

We are good friends, Ju-Ju and I, because we don't intrude on one another. Sometimes our being together is just an extension of each of us. If I look forward to seeing anyone, it's Ju-Ju. We never have to do a lot of reviewing; our friendship is continual.

Berrigan's Journal — December 23
I'm waiting at the train station for Syru. She's running final errands. Ju-Ju is good company but even he is rather subdued. Can a baby have melancholia? I'm nearly drowning in it. Tears impend with every remark. Emotions are so damn troublesome! Last night we were so dear; we came into ultimate contact with one another, as if our blood ran together and our breath drew in and out of both of us at the same time. And now we must comply with convention and family pilgrimage at Christmas. It's so ridiculous! Everyone is shallow; they don't recognize the pains of separation and absence. They struggle to make sporadic connections that might last until the next empty holiday reunion. It's not only an uncomfortable bore, but also one of the ultimate hypocrises.

LATER . . . How abandoned I felt as their train faded away from me, melting into the frosty evening darkness. Ju-Ju waved feebly; Syru could not manage it. The station house has a mocking coldness now, as it is invaded by the bustle and swish of package-laden Christmas travelers, hurrying to Yuletide hot toddies, choir programs, or their own awkward reunions. If I keep my mind on Ju-Ju's face when I gave him the bright red muffler, maybe I can endure the days until the New Year when they return to me. Walking back in the snow, I remember the first night Syru and I walked through the leaves. Alone, with the Bingham streetlamps flickering at me, I can let out my tears.

Phone call from Evelyn, an invitation for a pre-Christmas toast at BJ's. She's just the friend I need.

Berrigan's Journal — December 24
The house is astir with Christmas movement. Grandpa is asleep under yesterday's paper. Mom and Aunt Mildred are in the kitchen fussing goodnaturedly over the turkey and fixings. "Mother, you do a great Christmas spread," my father will pronounce after dinner, as he has done ever since I can remember. Then the men will retire to TV-watching or fast-action checkers while the women continue their work in cleaning the kitchen. Their relationships seem so flimsy to me; the men put little stock in all the patient careful cooking. They're naggingly nearsighted, overfed on insensitivity.

Some neighborhood friends come by . . . . my father's favorite nephew (the brother I never had, I suppose) is expected at the train station in several hours.

My Christmas toast with Evelyn was really pleasant, a resurrection of spirits after the ordeal at the train station. I gave her some of my poetry in a little book I made, with my own illustrations (including several erotic sketches for humor). I included copies of some of the letters Syru and I have exchanged because I know I can share them with Evelyn, and she'll be glad for me without intrusive questions. Her exchange was a sachet of scented flower petals. "I did this myself, Berrigan, saving all the goddamned daisy petals I could find, every used corsage at the sorority house and even some cherished roses from the housemother's private garden. Now *that's* friendship!" Both of us enjoyed our gifts over warm brandy near the fire in BJ's.

Evelyn was intrigued by our signatures in the letters as "Sappho" and "Diana."

"Someday these letters will be immortalized in good lesbian literature," she said. "From what I can tell about Syru, she's got Sappho's zeal and independent nature. And you as Diana, eternally virgin, protector of nymphs! It's the nymphs part you like best, I'm sure!

"The only thing that doesn't jibe is that you'd hardly make a good archer! Not if you handle a bow and arrow the same way you used to deal with kites. Remember all those things that crashed into the trees? I mean, the wrecked relics remain even to this day!

"But Berrigan, I hope you know I wish you the best with Syru. Just remember, you can turn to me for any help I can offer, whenever you need me. But I hope your life together goes well and you won't have to call for help. Of course, you can still call just to have coffee!" Then she hugged me, and we laughed, downed the brandy and celebrated our pasts and our less regal present.

The dinner bell rings, so I must march into the dining hall to look over that steaming turkey into the faces of people I've known all my life, those who understand me the least: my family.

Berrigan's Journal — December 25

Long distance to Syru, who is as miserable as I am. Ju-Ju sends a special gurgle to me over the phone. If I could just have him on my lap a few minutes! Syru assures me that the candle is always lighted, burning, a good luck omen for us.

Berrigan's Journal — December 27

A lonely day . . . . the hours are slow, until this letter at mailtime, an envelope unmistakenly addressed by Syru. Inside it, a piece of notebook paper with four pubic hairs taped to the page, and this message:

"You are the poet, I concede. But here are four lines of a new kind of poetry, shed from willing follicles, a kinky design of me as a woman on this page. A more female verse I could not attempt. Today I startled the ghosts of all dead lovers who ever sent love lockets by sitting nude in a graveyard, writing this to you. My nakedness has been different since you have seen me.

S. 'Sappho' "

Berrigan's Journal — December 31

Evelyn and I are going to bring in the New Year as we both prefer: not in some bar making chitchat with a lot of casual drunks, but at a Woody Allen film over a Superbox of buttered popcorn! I plan to add some adventure by concealing some beer underneath my coat!

This afternoon we were going through my closet and got hysterical trying on several of my prom formals. Evelyn suggested we wear those to the movie. I am eager for distraction and agreed. She smuggled them out of the house in a plastic garbage bag.

* * * * * *

The ticket takers at the Crown Theatre in Bingham were unprepared for Evelyn and Berrigan in their long gowns and spiked heels. "Some costume party prank, I bet," one of them remarked. The two friends were giggly as they chose their seats, having already consumed several cans of the beer. Berrigan had worn Evelyn's calf-length beaver coat; it had large pockets sewn inside so the beer was no trouble to conceal. They were beside themselves popping the tabs in the back row while Woody Allen endured his own bizarre plot.

When they emerged from the film near midnight, both were past the giggles and well into drunk and disorderly.

"We've go to do something outrageous," Evelyn insisted.

"I know juss the thing. Les go stomp my high school emblem!"

"What?"

"Iss sacred, see. Sposed to give the school sports good luck. And make all the athletes virile."

"Down with virility!"

"Can you spell that at this hour?"

"Sure, *V-U-R* . . . ."

"Never mind. Iss a ways so les getta car."

"You mean *steal* one!"

"No, juss borrow! *Les head for Steven Pinkley's."*

The allure of Steven Pinkley's car was the horn, which made an *"AA-OO-Gah"* sound that could be heard for blocks. It was Steven's pride and joy, this old jalopy. The car sat in his driveway, with blocks behind the wheels so it wouldn't roll. It was an old hand-crank model, but Steven had worked it over so that it would start on the first turn. Everyone in Bingham knew about it.

Berrigan wobbled up the dark street, her beaver coattails flapping. Evelyn followed; they were whispering a plan to each other frantically. At Pinkley's, all was quiet and dark, so Evelyn pulled the blocks out from behind the car. The two of them pushed it until it rolled out into the street, one of them also steering. Both the drive and the street were steep so they ran alongside the car, hopped on the side boards and finally made it in the car down at the bottom of the street's incline.

"Okay. Start 'er up!"

Steven's work paid off and the two women chugged along Maple Avenue up to Bingham High School. There in the moonlight on a grassy knoll they spied the sacred emblem. They ran jiggling and stumbling up the grass to the knoll, shaking the beer in progress. Evelyn popped a tab and the fizzy brew spewed up and over both of them in a sudsy shower. Berrigan began singing the Bingham High fight song, as she danced on the emblem, relishing the sacrilege. Evelyn danced with her, laughing until both of them slipped in the beer and fell over onto the emblem. They began slapping it like a tom-tom in a raucous rhythm, shouting "Go team go!"

Car lights appeared down the street so they scrambled up to get back in the car. Berrigan shook a can of beer and then placed it in the center of the emblem, fizzling like an alcoholic roman candle. She yelled, *"Drink 'em, shrink 'em, Bingham High!"* Their final salute to the desecrated emblem came in three harsh *"AA-OO-Gah's."*

Returning Steven Pinkley's beloved jalopy proved a tricky maneuver. Berrigan drove to the street one block over from the Pinkley's, shut off the engine and then coasted around the corner and into the drive. Evelyn jumped off to replace the blocks. She slipped on the side board, dropping her beer can, which rattled noisily into the street. A light went on in the Pinkley's and some-one called, "Who's out there? What's going on?"

The prom gowns were not cut for sprinting, but Berrigan and Evelyn hiked them up and did their best, exiting pronto into a nearby park. There, safe in the bushes, they panted and popped their final beer tab. "Welcome to the new year, crazy friend," they toasted.

Upon Syru's return to Bingham, there was little time for leisurely lovers' renewal. Convention plans spent the hours quickly. Berrigan found herself jockeying between three urgencies: her job at Amil's, caring for Ju-Ju to free Syru's time, and helping the NAW women prepare their panel. They had decided to expand on the rape prevention program they had given to Gamma Phi. Berrigan finally decided it would help if she gave up her own apartment and moved in with Syru. Though she was glad for the move, Syru was too preoccupied with her vision of the national convention to be overly enthusiastic.

Several days before they were scheduled to begin their car caravan towards Washington, Syru received a phone call from her husband. He told her that she would be receiving notice that he had filed for divorce. He insisted that they meet within the week to determine settlement with their attorneys. When she told him she could not schedule any meetings until after the convention, he grew angry and hostile.

"Oh yeah, I know about your women's lib activities. You better see to it that you get to these meetings or else I'm gonna file for custody too. All that equal rights crap might not sit so well with a judge, you know. Maybe times haven't changed as much as you think."

Syru was frantic, angry, on the brink of hysteria. She saw all the hard work and her chance to make national connections with other women falling rapidly away from her. Her hopes seemed dashed for rejuvenation in Washington in the company of other politically aware, radical feminists. When Berrigan arrived home from work to find Syru in this state, she could hardly make the story out. She was shocked to learn that Syru was still married to Ron Cox, and was hurt by Syru's lack of trust in sharing this information with her before. But she overlooked her own feelings to comfort her distraught lover.

An emergency NAW meeting was called. Syru explained her situation briefly and suggested that Berrigan become their panel leader and chapter spokeswoman. Berrigan felt in a quandary: which was more important? To be the one substitute at convention Syru would trust or to be with Syru for her settlement meetings? She wished she would receive the answers by Quick Service mail from karmic headquarters, wished for a red conference telephone connected to Doris's office. She wished for a carrier pidgeon from Lesbos, even though none of these fantasies revealed an answer for her decision. She could take Ju-Ju to the convention but it would be hard for Syru to find her if she needed her. On the other hand, Syru was determined to go to the meetings alone. Berrigan wanted to insure Ju-Ju's care and bolster Syru, yet she too was disappointed at the prospect of missing the convention. Personal and public politics seemed to conflict, or else Berrigan couldn't see clearly how they connected. She finally chose to decline Syru's suggestion of her as spokeswoman. She would stay in Bingham with Ju-Ju.

Back at home, Syru was in a fury. Berrigan couldn't decide what made her most angry: missing the convention or the fact that Cox, who could not leave her when they were married, filed first for divorce. She was unconsoleable, unreachable. She stomped through the rooms, kicking at things. She was angry at Cox, at the loose ends of a life she couldn't forget, at her own feelings, at the jubilation of the NAW women over the convention. Taking refuge, Ju-Ju curled quietly in a corner of his crib. Finally Berrigan could not bear the distress any longer. She went into the bedroom where Syru was sitting on the fire escape, banging her boots against the metal.

"Syru," she called too softly. *"Syru, you've got to stop this!"* Startled, the other woman turned to her, her face taut with anguish. Her armor split wide open in an explosion only the two of them could hear. She put out her arms and said, "Berrigan, come hold me. I need some of your strength now."

* * * * * *

They all met in a parking lot on the edge of Bingham: the NAW women ready to drive to the convention in Washington, Syru on her way to New York for the settlement meetings. Berrigan held Ju-Ju, who, not recognizing the subtleties in mood, drooled good-naturedly. They all hugged each other, raised their fists in salute to sisterhood, wished each other good luck. The other women knew how upset Syru was; they wished to offer her their solace but didn't know what to say. She preferred to pretend that warriors never show pain or weakness. Berrigan chafed at the restrictive defensive poses everyone seemed to hide behind. As they drove away, waving, she felt herself empty out as parts of her went with each of them in different directions.

The next few days were agonizingly long. Berrigan was alone and lonely, buffeted by the phone ringing at all hours. It was either Syru or someone from Washington calling about Syru. Syru would cry and tell her how ugly Cox was being. He ranted and raved about all the things she'd done in the past that he could never stand. He called her crazy, unreliable, a poor mother. He implied he suspected her a lesbian. He bickered over distribution of their plastic dishes. He told the lawyers she didn't let him see his son. She was furious and hurt; Berrigan could do so little for her over the phone.

The women in Washington wanted news of Syru. Berrigan could hear the voices of eager conversation in the background. They bubbled with energy, giving her synopses of the panels they attended, the terrific speakers they heard, the constant dialogues. Berrigan could hear when they spoke that something had broken open inside of them. They had seen 4,000 other women ready to change the world with them and something new was blooming.

Finally at the end of the week, the phone rang at 2:00 A.M., jolting Berrigan from her restless dreams. She thought fleetingly of tearing it from the wall. She was surrounded by black space, discarded baby shoes, pages of yesterday's newspaper. The phone rang again and again. It was Syru. The meetings were finished.

"The bastard kept me from convention, signed all the papers and then ran off to leave *me* to see the judge. I'm on the docket for tomorrow at nine. Thank god my lawyer knew who to bribe to get me on this quick. I'll be home by five."

The hours waiting for Syru's return were nerve-wracking. From their brief phone conversation, Berrigan could only gauge that her lover was tired, boneweary with sorting out the scattered relics of a marriage gone awry. When finally she came through the door, Berrigan went immediately to her, tried to console her. But Syru would receive no touching or words of comfort. She had been betrayed by circumstance and Ron Cox in a way only she could understand. Her chance to share her outrage and rub elbows with other revolutionary women had slipped past her. Fate was her enemy and everyone Fate's agent. She had been denied her audience, just when she felt her energies peaking. No other time would be as right for her.

They sat at the kitchen table, Syru ignoring her cocoa. She had told Berrigan nothing about seeing the judge. Suddenly she began.

"He had this absolutely righteous expression on his face, this 'god, I'm a busy and important person' attitude about him. You know what he said to me? After all the little bullshit double-checking information questions like names, addresses, dates and crap — he looks at me from behind the sanctity of his precious legal title and he says, 'Are you absolutely sure you want this divorce?'

"I wanted to press his fat little righteous nose flat against his moralistic face. I bored him, you understand? My wretched divorce took up his time. He had to deal with the last trappings of my pitiful past and it irritated him! I wanted to puke, right in his lap, right on his robe, right on his oh-so-distinctly inked paperwork!"

Berrigan's Journal — January 25

There is slim possibility that Syru and I will be as content as we were those few months before her divorce. Like two wheels rolling together, we're stranded with crucial cogs broken irreparably. I try to keep faith and appear cheery and heartened, but something essential in her has dissolved. Although her anger is gone, it's replaced by a maelstrom of melancholy. Nothing offers her restoration. She's not purposely rude to me or unmindful of Ju-Ju, but all her primary drives are numb. When I attempt to make love to her, she responds half-heartedly, almost apologetically. She plays with Ju-Ju, but is out of his realm, and he knows they are not in contact.

It's hard for me to comprehend that her absence at the convention could create this undiminishing depression, but she won't talk about it, or let me know her thoughts. She must have seen it as her own personal Valhalla.

Our sisters return from Washington almost as different women, full of a drive only Syru has had before. They are excited about new ideas and programs. They are full of information, talking non-stop. When they ask Syru about her divorce, she side steps detail, saying only that it is finished with no problems. There is something sweet in the gentle way they try to coax her back to her vociferous self, something shy but strong. They have brought her back badges and flyers from the convention. Now she has the trinkets; I just wish she had the feeling.

Berrigan's Journal — February 10

The picture is not as dim as I thought. Syru's trauma eases and she shows signs of revival. Her reaction time is nearly back to normal, her interest in Ju-Ju and me more real. But she's still on the fringes of a daze, dropping in and out of her mind-ways.

In the past several weeks, she's begun again her involvement with NAW, exhilarated to be "back at the line," especially with all the new programs the women are initiating. They came to her with the idea of buying a building for a women's center, and need her as Super-Sister to get funding through PR with businesses.

Meanwhile, I'm defaulted into a role I never expected to fill of my own volition: mother and housewife. But for me, Ju-Ju would founder under the crusts of breakfast-past, the beds would mold with muss. A woman who chooses to make a home with children must love the avocation, beating incredible risk of failure. Domesticity is made of dramas the size of pinpoints; everyday life is not glamorous.

Berrigan's Journal — February 14

Coming out of her self-absorption, Syru celebrated with me on this traditional lover's day. She gave me a silver pendant, in the design of an upraised fist inside the symbol of woman. Ju-Ju played contentedly, watching as we made love on his blanket just out of reach of the playpen. Syru was startled at the point of climax when a teddy-bear bounced off her chest. We laughed and started over again, almost glad for the interruption; it gave us a renewed beginning.

We have not loved like this — relaxed, as friends, a family — in a long time. But it made Valentine's day so much more than the traditional huge heart-shaped box of candy wrapped in sterile cellophane, colored the red of Fifties lipstick.

Evelyn did not forget me. She's been over several times when Ju-Ju and I were here alone. I've enjoyed her company, doing the laundry, joking away the drudgery. She's also been invaluable help with all the hand-work involved in folding flyers, stapling,

58

cutting, addressing envelopes for NAW mailings. She's uncommitted but inquisitive, asking me how I feel about the ERA, what I think it will do for women.

"I'm afraid the only thing that equal rights implies for the women of Gamma Phi is that the guys get to take the pill instead of them!"

Today when Evelyn knew Syru and I would be together, she sent a package in her place. Inside it, a red and white fuzzy dog: sad-eyed, droopy tail. It held the attached card in its mouth:

"Barking this message on Valentine's Day — hurry up and pass the ERA!" The card is safe here in these pages, but the fluffy dog was less fortunate. Ju-Ju popped its fuzzy head into his mouth at once, and drowned it in delighted gurgling.

Something transient about this day, as if it's been a dream. Only Evelyn seems real. And Ju-Ju, who diplomatically reminds me that it's way past his dinner hour.

I lose Syru; she's off to an ERA committee meeting. Sometimes there are no traces of her in the house and I wonder, *"Does she really live with us?"*

Berrigan's Journal – February 23

Excitement is brewing. The NAW women have located a house we can afford to buy and renovate as a Women's Center. Jan is heading a committee to put lumber and construction suppliers on the spot, letting them do penance with donated materials. Margaret has worked in the city commissioner's office and is checking out NAW's applying for city funds as a community service organization. But the best possibility for long-range funding has come through a contact of Elaine's. A friend of hers is the wife of a company president. He heads the largest insurance agency in Connecticut and is willing to divest some money to the Center for a tax deduction. We all joked about this being "guilt financing."

At first Syru was skeptical, questioning if the wife had any consciousness or if the NAW project was just on a par with garden club. Elaine told her she was too suspicious. Syru's tack turned onto the husband.

"What's in this for him? For his company? Suddenly it's very 'in' to give money to women. Somehow it's supposed to assuage all the old grievances."

Delia countered, "Who cares about their motives? You've always told us we let The Man rip us off; here's our chance to really do something for women on The Man's money. I say take him for all he's worth!"

"Just as long as there are no strings attached," Syru insisted. "All agreed?"

The other women agreed and even though all of us will be at the meeting with the company representatives, Syru was urged to act as official NAW spokeswoman.

"Just get them to pledge us the moon, Syru, that's all we ask!"

I confess to harboring resentment of Syru now. She hasn't tried to include me in her new burst of feminist dedication, as she originally did when we met. And after I've tried to be a sister and support her, offer friendship as well as my love. It's hard for me to sit back and be silent while she forges new directions. Her respect for the freedom within our relationship is forgotten.

It seems that I should just naturally be supportive of her, even if my own development and expression suffers in the process. She doesn't really see me as part of NAW, but as an appendage of herself. The situation is intolerable and requires that I ignore my own needs.

I haven't rebelled yet because what is happening to Ju-Ju takes precedence. What pitiful little he asks, yet Syru rejects any dependence, no matter how small. He has become weepy, sleeps fitfully, is easily upset and nervous. Ever watchful for Syru, he jerks for the door at the slightest sound. Going against my principles, I've written Syru's mother, explaining in the clearest terms I could all the circumstances, and asking if she would take Ju-Ju, or at least talk to Syru about him.

A showdown for us is imperative, but how I dread confrontation! And especially with Syru, whom I admire and love, but who takes from me too casually. I dread the argument, the conflict, but greater is my dread of these days on end with no communication, co-habiting in emotional limbo, while Ju-Ju withers.

* * * * * *

Bright and early on the following Wednesday morning, the hopeful women arrived one by one at the insurance company offices. They gathered in the lounge, buoyant on the soft pile carpeting, soothed and seated in the well-padded art deco chairs. With scattered conversation, they waited for Syru and Berrigan, waited to be called in to meet the company president and his marketing manager. Alice touched at her hair; Margaret wondered if the pantsuit she'd sewn from a pattern was cut right in the shoulders. They all assured each other of success.

When Syru did arrive, the other women huddled around her, eager to share their nervous energy, urging her, "be sure to ask for . . . ." In the midst of this, president Jim Biggs came out of his office. With one sweep of his hand as invitation, the twelve NAW members were ushered into his office and then on into the executive conference room.

Ghosts of previous high-level bull sessions lingered like cobwebs in the corners of the room. The chairs and table were solid oak, heavy and highly sheened: tasteful, professional, masculine, important. The women were duly impressed. Syru leaned over and whispered to Berrigan as they were seated, "I'm ready for a seance with all this Gothic furniture." Berrigan winked back.

60

Introductions were served with coffee. Bob Beren then presented a short explanation of the company, its advertising image, and statistics on their women policy holders. His hair was expertly parted in the middle, his suit entirely buttoned down and dapper. He concluded, saying, "When we're all done here, maybe some of you might want to think about our plan. We'll write you a check, and then you can write one for us!"

His joke elicited polite laughter. President Biggs took over then, leaning one shoulder hard into the massive chair and speaking with a practiced air of informal authority. He told the women that the stockholders of his company were progressive and encouraged equal opportunity hiring even without a state ERA.

"We've hired three women agents in the last six months," he announced proudly. Syru shifted uneasily in her chair, not impressed with his condescending attitude.

The other women, except for Delia, listened to Bigg's diatribe attentively, sipping their coffee from matching ceramic mugs. Delia nudged Berrigan. "I bet he's great in his training films!" Berrigan feigned a yawn and Syru scowled at both of them.

Biggs concluded with fatherly forbearance: "I'll be honest with you. We stand to gain a tax break and some good advertising with our donation to your Center. You stand to gain a nice fat bank balance. That seems like a fair exchange to do us both some good." He smiled, raising his coffee cup as a toast and sipping from it loudly.

"There are some questions of policy and operation we'd like to discuss briefly," Beren told them. Syru sat up a little straighter; her radar had snapped on.

"Nothing too detailed. We'd just like an outline of your goals, some of the programs you'll be sponsoring. That sort of thing." Mr. Biggs was still smiling and sipping.

"I've got that all laid out here," Delia offered. Beren and Biggs skimmed the Center goals and structure outline quickly.

"Simple but solid," Beren remarked.

"Nothing out of the ordinary that I can see," Biggs added.

Berrigan began to feel uncomfortable about something in the atmosphere of the meeting that she couldn't pinpoint, an expectancy, an "on the verge" sensation. When she looked at Syru, she realized she was monitoring her lover's emotional level. As Syru seemed about to speak, Beren said, "Don't you think we can discuss the amount of our pledge now, Jim?" Everyone at the table leaned in just a bit, focusing on Biggs and the figure he was about to announce.

But his attention had swung back to the program listing for the Center. "I wonder," he said, running his finger down the list, "if you aren't starting out with just a little too much *diversity*." None of the women responded; most of them shifted their eyes from Biggs to Syru. She was pausing long enough to try to gauge his meaning.

61

Beren felt the awkward hesitance and tried his managerial skills at loosening the mood.

"I don't think either Jim or I want to try telling you how to run your Center . . . ." Biggs tossed the list onto the table, silencing his co-worker.

"Ladies," he began, "don't worry. You're going to get your money. But I love a good political argument. And I have some very pointed questions about this Center that I want answered!"

What ensued as a result of Mr. Biggs' questions was a scene no one had expected when they filed into the conference room. For the following hour, he and Syru were deadlocked in a battle of wits that started politely enough but ended in a shouting match. The other women had thought that the meeting was only a formality. None of them had suspected that Biggs had his own political opinions and one way or another, he was going to try and donate them to the Center right along with his money. No one had estimated the wisdom of Syru's warning about accepting company funding with "no strings attached."

Biggs suggested firmly that there were "radical forces" which he expected not to be entertained at the Women's Center. He hedged on defining that term when Syru pressed him. He suggested the danger of becoming "too intense about politics," and kept mentioning "community opinion" about the Center. The confounding thing about him was that he refused to say anything directly, but held to an absolute and adamant rightness in his carefully-worded allusions.

Delia tried valiantly to calm everyone down but finally Syru had heard enough. She exploded all over Biggs with 33 years of her rage and rhetoric. The attack was so hard and fast that she silenced everyone and left the room echoing with her anger.

"Radical forces? Do you mean women who don't want to stay home with the kids anymore? Students? Commies? Prostitutes? Women who are pro-abortion? Women willing to come out in the open and talk about their husbands beating them? Do you mean lesbians? When I leave this room *without* your check, I go out to work for and with *all* these women. You can remember this day as a first. A real live revolutionary radical lesbian sat in this chair, listened to your bullshit, and refused your money."

Syru's desire to shock Biggs succeeded, but so did it also stun the women she considered her allies. As Margaret tried to salvage some connecting point, "This has all gotten out of hand," Biggs ignored her and adjourned the meeting. Everything had gone to pieces unexpectedly and the women trailed out of the office in a daze of confusion, anger, surprise.

Berrigan's Journal – March 7

NAW meeting tonight in an uproar. First everyone was squabbling, claiming ignorance, trying to blame Syru for ruining the money deal on the Center. But that passed, leaving us in a shamble of jangled feelings. No one is as mad at Syru or as upset about her lesbian declarations as we are at ourselves. We set up a dream that some of us thought would instantly come true, fueled on convention fervor and a little of The Man's money. Most of my friends, these women rallying behind the NAW banner, are just now realizing The Man is real and Syru hasn't been squawking garbage at us all this time. None of us knew what to say to Mr. Biggs and Mr. Beren as they subtly and unsubtly manipulated our dream. We all wanted to use Syru as a shield from that and when she wasn't diplomatic, we weren't sure whether to be mad at her or them. We want our Center and our politics too and we want it all now, without having to fight or hurt anyone's feelings.

Unfortunately, Syru doesn't read our doubt as self-doubt but only as a vote of no-confidence in her. She is more angry than when she missed convention, is hurt by her own misconception of our feelings and yet will not share this. She is aloof, pretending again that the only thing she feels is political, not personal. She dismissed us, scathing in her disappointment. "They pushed and you all turned into Barbie Dolls."

Alice whines, feeling guilty, "We should have talked about the lesbian thing before." I wonder if she's worried Mr. Biggs will see her at the grocery store and raise his eyebrows quizzically, lasering her sprouting consciousness with his silent question: "Are you one too?"

Elaine apologizes for being a willing follower, for admiring Syru's zeal, and yet accepting her own inclination to let someone else lead and make all the decisions.

We're drained and we come to no conclusions or analysis of the meeting. I think each of us wanted to tell Syru we were sorry for being angry with her, but our pride, guilt, or fear gets in the way. We feel foolish. She's still the only strong one, it seems.

I feel sorry for myself, for my friends in this NAW group, and for Syru. I doubt she can be salvaged back to us now. We have censured her with our confusion and she is unforgiving. We all have a different dilemma which I understand. And yet, I have my own with Syru, which is personal, political, painful . . . . my love for Syru is not her answer, no aid now when her dreams and goals seem in ashes. We have both paid dearly for our lessons; I know Syru loves me but she loves the illusive feminist dream more, and clings to her own protective defenses more dearly than she ever has clung to me. I was never her beacon or inspiration, anymore than I can now be her sanctuary.

Berrigan's Journal — March 11
Syru left the meeting before I did, leaving the rest of us staring dumbly at each other, wondering what will happen now. I walked for awhile, returning to Bingham Square, hearing the echoes of the

NAW women as I first saw them at their ERA rally. I half wished I could go get Amil's bottle stashed at the back of the store to escape the evening. I walked to the Gamma Phi house and threw some pebbles up against Evelyn's window but all was dark and quiet.

When I went back to the apartment, Syru was at the kitchen table, her head bent over a cocoa cup, silhouetted in the light, a sight so familiar to me. I wanted to go and cradle that head in my arms, kiss her hair . . . . but she shuns intimacy with all the passion she never shares in other things.

We talked then, without touching, reviewing our time together. Parts of me were twanging with righteous outrage. She took me for granted, left me repeatedly as Ju-Ju's guardian, believed assumptions about our relationship. She grew defensive and upset when I tried to talk to her about Ju-Ju's needs. She called me a martyr.

I said she had changed, had left off loving all of me. *"You love me when I'm folding leaflets and willing to march. But you don't love me when I have a different opinion from yours or when I want more of you than an exciting political discussion. Ju-Ju can't complain about that kind of conditional love, but I can. We used to talk, Syru, we were friends, then lovers. We used to be much bigger women then we are now.*

"It is one thing to work shoulder to shoulder for a cause; but any effort for anything greater than we are is empty, if we do not work heart to heart as well."

When I finished saying these things to Syru, I also reminded her of our early days together, times when she was more willing to relax, to make love without desperation. She put her head down and sighed, raising her face up then to look at me and speak in a flat voice, weary, tinged with defeat.

"Sometimes I'm afraid. So I have this tunnel vision which gets me through, but it keeps me from seeing my own demons, my own faults. I've got this idea of what lies at the end of the tunnel and I'm going for it, at whatever cost. It's got to be better. Everyone else is studying how the light varies along the path. I'm just a miner, I guess, boring past everything and everyone, in the process of making a hole in the world that doesn't end in nothing. But I can't protect anyone else: not you, not Ju-Ju. Besides, I don't owe you that. You have to learn the very first thing about being a woman: the idea that someone else will take care of you is the oldest lie."

Syru looked helplessly at me but wouldn't come to me. I began to cry in small short shakes and then my tears were uncontrollable. I knew I wasn't going to come out of our relationship with her, and I had to come out with what was left of me. She started to go, then turned back and got something off the bookcase, put it on the table in front of me, and went out the door. It was the silver candlesnuffer.

* * * * *

64

Berrigan's Journal — March 13

Syru has been gone since Wednesday. Her mother is coming to get Ju-Ju today. I can't stay here for him or for myself any longer. I've decided to leave: destination unknown. I just know I have to leave Bingham for a while. There's bad karma here for me; two relationships have foundered and I can't afford strike three. Not here, not now.

Evelyn, as always my friend and confidante, has loaned me $200 until I get relocated. If only Syru would come back, I might try again to explain some of my feelings to her. But she won't answer to anyone else's call. I guess that's as it must be.

Certain moments run over me and I get rushes of hysteria, I go awash with despair and loneliness. What a bugaboo: self pity!

Syru has left it all: working for the Women's Center, the child she created with her ultimate womanpower, the books, the hanging candle I gave her for Christmas, and our love. Did it matter so little? Where can she be?

Well, I hope you are alive and well, Syru Cox, wherever you are, Woman Warrior at large and raging. My mercy is divided between you with your pain, and the world which must contain you.

Berrigan's Journal — March 15

Ju-Ju has gone with his grandmother; my belongings except for what I have in my shoulder bag and backpack, are stored safely with Evelyn. Sitting here, looking out the window of an empty apartment, I see that Bingham is the same as it has always been and does not shift sympathetically with changes in my melodrama.

A strange thing happened. As I was writing this entry, an envelope slid under the door. When I opened the door, no one was there, but going back to the window, I saw Syru walking rapidly down the street away from the apartment, the knot of hair in the back of her bandana bobbing away from me, out of my reach forever.

Inside the envelope this message:

" 'Diana':

I am still me. I cannot change or deny the things I've done with us, with the NAW sisters, with myself. I go where I am going, almost predestined. But I loved you, even though impatiently or ungently. Be well, please take care. Thank you for seeing to Ju-Ju.

S. 'Sappho' "

* * * * * *

(Gwan away from Bingham town,
Bad vibes here have put me down.
Gwan away, gwan away,
off and out to who-knows-where,
see what I can find out there.)

Berrigan's Journal — March 20
My week hitching rides ends. I have chanced as many unknown roads as I can on this trip. My bones refuse to wander any further; my brain is furry with loneliness. A flashing sign at the edge of the city blinked at me and I answered, *"Hello St. Louis. My name is Berrigan."*

Chapter 5

Telegram for Evelyn Walker, March 27:
*"Am in St. Louis. Got small apartment on Foxglove Street.
Job hunting five days: no luck. May have to resort to ye ole
secretarialism! Thanks again for everything, especially
yourself. Don't worry about me. Will call you when I get a
phone.*
                              Love, Berrigan."

Berrigan's Journal — April 10
Approaching Spring is the only reason for good humor in St.
Louis today. I have finally found a job, but I'm not sure I can last
long enough to get my first paycheck. I think I'm not cut out to
spend my hours of daylight inside, twenty stories high, cultivating
the friendship of manila folders and the IBM Executive which can
do all manner of witty typing tricks. The buzz of phones, telex bills,
the rumble of coffee carts: such is the music of the business world
(as well as the peculiar piped in music in *this* office: organ melodies
bordering on the funereal). But all my other job hunting attempts
came up empty, so I've settled temporarily for Secretary to the
Associate Producer at Kingline Industries.

Kingline produces advertising and training films. The only
problem is that there are *twelve* Associate Producers, and most of
them really don't do any significant work from what I can tell.
They're just one more group of paper shufflers.

My job interview had the inane dialogue of an Albee sketch.
By the end of it, I felt like one of Dali's clocks, flattened of all
dimension, sliding over the edge of reality, into the insanity of
reality.

"Good day, I'm Mr. Johnson, Associate Producer #10 here at
Kingline. And you're . . . . (with a pallid smile, he fumbled for my
application) Berrigan?"

"Yes."

"Would you like to smoke?"

"No, thank you."

"Would you like to cross your legs? Can you type 60 words per
minute? Does your bust-line match your IQ? Do you file left-
handed? What's the 14th letter in the alphabet? Do you have
asthma? Are you near-sighted? A virgin? A Scorpio? Do you gossip? Do you sleep in the nude? Do you squeeze the Charmin? What's
this deal about short hair?" (he raises his eyebrows and gives my

hair the once-over) "Have you read *The Sensuous Woman?* I see you write marital status as 'Ms.' But are you in fact married? Or are you one of those 'bra-burners?' " (he chuckled, as though he'd got my goat).

"No sir. 'Fruit of the Looms' really burn better. They ignite faster, I understand."

"So what's your favorite cartoon show? 'Superwoman,' I suppose?"

"No, 'Super Heroes,' actually. All the female voices are done by men. Naturally the love scenes are the best."

After contemplating me in my short hair and my well-manufactured, unflinching confidence (a total bluff), Mr. Johnson proved surprising.

"Signed, sealed, and delivered: the job is yours, on the basis of your sense of humor. You'll need that to survive at Kingline."

I checked myself in with the Controller (who looks like a prison warden) and headed for my work area. I was accompanied through these greeting formalities by a rotund, bespectacled, ambitious Associate Producer's Assistant. His assignment was to show me around the building, but he was more interested in his own monologue on Kingline miscellany.

"Mr. Wayne, the Controller, isn't a bad guy," the assistant-guide told me, "so long as you know how to get on his good side."

Passing a door marked *"Darkroom, film in processing,"* my guide offered what I'm sure he thought sage advice.

"If you ever need a little privacy . . . . you know, for any cheek-to-cheek discussions, that's the place to go."

When we parted company at the door to the steno area where I would be working, the assistant's braggadocio dissolved, and his hesitance suggested we had reached the entrance to "no man's land."

"See you around," he called, edging rapidly back down the hall. "Oh! Listen, if there's anything you need to know or find out, just ask me. I'm Ronald Prince, and I work for Mr. Dower. Extension 51!" With that, he raced around the corner and out of sight.

For a moment when I walked in to the steno area, there was a break in the clickety clackety of the faithful IBM's. The office "girls" sized me up in a quick bi-focaled glance, then their steady hum of production resumed. I had arrived, been seen, categorized, and mentally filed.

I have resigned myself to this job for the time being, spending my lunch hours reading the want-ads in hopes I'll find something else; guess I may even end up with a paper route or driving a fork lift!

I'm trying hard to keep up with my writing at night, after work. Short of having Evelyn with me, my writing is the best friend I brought from Bingham. But now all too often I lose myself to the past, indulging in melancholy, reliving my loss of Syru, as if re-enacting the pain again and again will somehow purge me of the reality of my own loneliness. I miss Ju-Ju's jolly presence.

* * * * * *

Berrigan's impression of the Kingline Controller had been accurate. Jack Wayne regulated office procedure exactly like a warden, issuing "plan of action" memos and supervising the extension of secretarial duties to keeping two multicup coffee urns full at all times. He would insist that the refreshment area be kept neat. In his favorite platitude, he would incessantly declare, "Here at Kingline, we like to keep everything *well-spiffed.*" Possibly Jack Wayne was a genius in office management theory and his intelligence for figures uncanny. But his approach to people was unimag inative. At Volume Level Loud and Pitch Level High, he never *communicated:* he ordered, demanded, importuned, and remonstrated.

"Human beings are working machines!" Jack Wayne shouted in Berrigan's nightmares. It was by way of Berrigan, after several run-ins with Wayne on trivial matters of "procedure," that his nickname, "Warden Wayne," began to circulate.

The corporate octopus — Berrigan found herself lost among the tentacles of the business bureaucracy where the pomp and circumstance of "executivism" parades without conscience or concern for the common employee. Not only was adjustment to job surroundings and the Kingline system difficult, but Berrigan immediately saw that she would have to stay in the closet at work. But because of her immediate need for money, she was willing to temporarily submerge her gay pride.

In Bingham, she has always been able to be herself, even despite the fact that her family lived there. Here she was not on home ground, and she would have to play by new rules. In addition, the ache of loneliness plagued her; even for all her negative passions, Syru was a restless constant memory. Caught up in a dichotomy, Berrigan had to deny her real self, lie to those she worked with, and yet not lie to herself.

This was not an easy time for Berrigan . . . . memories nourished unfriendly melancholy during many lonely evenings in her little apartment on Foxglove Street. Syru was not out of her system; Berrigan often found herself at the bookcase, re-reading passages from Syru's favorite books, or remembering how they had danced to the song of revolution in a Bingham intersection.

Berrigan's Journal — April 18
I've been at Kingline long enough to begin examining the atmosphere, peering and sifting through all the doubletalk, no-talk, small-talk. Of particular interest are signs posted on the bulletin board in the employee lounge; they are metaphors of the absurd. It's clear to me they're aimed at the office "girls." Some of these gems read:

69

"Help your neighbor. Do your fair share, and part of hers."

"Every word you type is worth its weight in gold. Corporate time is money."

"Give that extra inch. It might take the Company that extra mile." They progress to the unbearable:

"The office is really just your home away from home."

"Executives are friends behind big desks."

"Our Company President is never inaccessible to his employees, especially if they have enthusiasm, new ideas, or a good fish story!"

The secretarial staff does little to buck their low-woman-on-the-totem-pole status. Several of their desk placards read:

"I'm not stupid — just lazy!"

"There all kinds of 'Working Girls'!"

"Do it now! (Big Brother May be Watching!)"

Perverse office humor; everyone presents themselves as a big joke, but no one is laughing.

The want-ads still do not offer me an alternative. In addition to the general office mania at Kingline, I've been visited several times by the obnoxious assistant who showed me around my first day, Ronald Prince.

"Just a personal follow-up," he explained, drooling on my desk. "If there's anything I can help you with here at Kingline, I am eager to be of service." Patting my knee knowingly, he left me to my secretaria. He's called three times this week to invite me to coffee and although I refused, I know he's not easily discouraged. Just what I need!

* * * * * *

From her few contacts with other secretaries, Berrigan perceived they were discontent but had invested too much to openly protest any of the unfair conditions surrounding them. Many of them depended on their jobs to support families, or had been with Kingline too long to risk their overdue promotion prospects by questioning office policy. Like a mandate from God, edicts out of Warden Wayne's office commanded their attention and obedience. But in secret, the women took verbal whacks at the corporate administration, although usually in hushed tones.

"Supervisors haunt the halls here, no place is safe," one woman told Berrigan.

Sitting directly across from Berrigan, as secretary to the Head of Distribution, was the formidable figure of Almagore Houston. Everyone called her Alma, but her tactics had earned her the secret nickname, "Gory." Alma was obsessed with *"Priority."* Her letters had to go through the postage meter first; her copies on the Xerox interrupted any and every other project there; hers was the very first cup of coffee out of the pot in the morning — *every* morning. Heaven help that innocent soul wanting coffee if Alma hadn't had her morning first: the count of trampled employees and stained clothing was high.

With Kingline nearly twelve years, Alma was close to the top. There was no chance she'd ever be the President's secretary, but her boss was a key Kingline man so she felt elevated above the rest of the secretaries. Almagore Houston was no mere "Associate Producer's girl." She was high on the totem pole, and let everyone know it.

Alma was too well endowed with idiosyncracies, odd twitchings, and a nagging bitchiness, enunciated in a whine and effected with a certain unconquerable bullishness. She baited the other women with a daily dose of sarcasm, tempered with calculated seiges of sweetness, compliments, gossipy chats, the occasional favor. None of her Kingline sisters were convinced, however. They knew this behavior only too well, having long since keyed in on Alma's strategy. Whenever she needed help, she selected a victim and approached, rattling a can of dry-roasted peanuts so that the nuts went round and round, almost like a warning sound. Every pitch for help started the same, in Gory's best tones of feigned congeniality.

"I was thinking . . . . if you're not too busy to help the Head of Distribution, second in command, you know . . . ." rattle, rattle, rattle.

Being unmarried made sharp-nosed Miss Houston the butt of office jokes and gossip. When she seemed cheery, all sorts of lurid suppositions were offered in explanation. First year Psych students looking for an example of the "Old Maid Syndrome" might easily have chosen Almagore to study. Berrigan always braced when she saw the dry-roasted peanuts coming her way; it meant added work, and a nasty confrontation that might leave Alma in tears if Berrigan refused to help.

And yet, despite Alma's irritating selfishness and bullying, whenever Berrigan overheard the spiteful jokes about her, she was not convinced that "Dear Ole Gory" was the enemy. Alma did not post the sexist slogans nor write Kingline policy. She followed it with a twelve-year allegiance to the company, her investment now more important than ever because she was near retirement age and would find it difficult to work elsewhere. Inconsiderate, ugly, rude, alone: these she clearly was. But many things make women bitter and harsh, Berrigan decided, easily including angry men who boss, and hateful jokes that even filter through the careful guards of corporate rank.

Ronald Prince often seemed to be a ringleader for the joksters, but his jabs were not pointed at Gory alone; he also contrived satirical rhymes flavored with sexual innuendo about many of the executives. His confidence in the effect these remarks would have if overheard seemed to stem from some inside information. Berrigan concluded that Ronald was in charge of Gossip Collection at Kingline.

71

Excluding Gory, most of the women at Kingline kept to themselves; there was little nonsense in their 8-to-5 regimen, except the lunch-hour gripe sessions. Berrigan didn't manage to make friends with many of them. Though they all seemed pleasant and willing to help, Berrigan picked up a signal of closure with each of them at a certain point.

"Stop. No Trespassing. Do not come any closer."

Kingline atmosphere stifled intimacy or even a hint of sisterhood. Such was not conducive to stretching the corporate inch into the corporate mile. Everyone seemed brainwashed by the same philosophy.

Fortunately, Berrigan did find another secretary willing to attempt friendship. Like Berrigan, Jade worked for an Associate Producer. She had been at Kingline only eight months and so had escaped the indoctrination of hard-core corporate loyalty which put blinders on many of the other women.

There was a free-wheeling love-of-life quality about Jade that didn't balk when Kingline procedure subjected her to being ignored, insulted, and skeptically observed. She went right on being unabashedly herself: coming to work braless, in togas and gypsy skirts, high boots and harem pants, reading "Muscle Man Magazine" in the john for shock value, and "Dr. Strange" comics for enjoyment.

Berrigan and Jade recognized in each other that they were partners in mutiny to the tyranny of the Korporate Kaptains. Their friendship made lunch hours and breaks tolerable, and Jade was uninhibited about sharing tips for survival.

"The Associate Producers suffer from mutant egos," she told Berrigan. "All of them secretly dream of careers directing porno films!"

"Here at Kingline, we are witnessing the war between the petty business bourgeoisie and the free thinkers," Jade was telling Berrigan at lunch one day.

"But where are the free thinkers? When do they show themselves? I suspect the bourgeoisie are winning the war at this point."

"Ah, but that's just it! It's a guerilla war! All the free thinkers are in disguise!"

"Except you. . .You're clearly an officer!"

"Oh, Berrigan, you're just jealous that I go braless and you won't."

"No one could tell if I did! Besides, I'm not sure I could handle all the attention you're getting as 'Queen of the tie-dyed nipple works!' "

"If you call Ronald Prince and his bulging eyeballs 'attention,' then I'm not impressed. But take heart; the latest Playboy poll says small breasted women are more sensual anyway! Really, Berrigan, I mean it. There are more women than us at Kingline who hate the **bullshit** memos and Warden Wayne's fetish for 'procedure.' "

"Oh yeah? Who?"

"Feddy Logan, for one."

"Who's she?"

"She works up on fourth floor, in Advertising. I've heard her raise hell about the anti-woman material that gets into some of the Kingline programs."

"Big deal. Three against a staff of . . . . What? 200? 300?"

"No, that's not all! Haven't you heard about the *real* war, between the FR's and the FD's?"

"All I've heard about is Gory's vibrator and using the darkroom for a lunchtime screw."

"More news from the notorious Ronald Prince again. He doesn't know anything about the darkroom. He's just hoping."

"He should be so lucky. But what's this about a real war?"

"FR, that's Film Requisition, is a department that gets all the orders for materials, films, etc. The orders are then written up as proposals, which go to the Head of FD-Film Distribution. That's David Andrews, Gory's boss. Naturally, every proposal crosses Gory's desk on the way to Andrews. Somewhere along the line, she appointed herself Official Censor and only too frequently proposals she doesn't like or requisitions from some person out of her favor never reach Andrews. Then he gives FR hell.

"But about six months ago, FR got a new director who's been waging battle with Gory. The new director delivers all the proposals by hand, directly to Andrews, never even recognizes Gory's existence. God, it makes the old bag burn! FR brings proposals up once a month; Gory is on a terror those days. She's full of more ammonia than a breakaway shit wagon loose on a steep hill! But it's worth it to see her put down. No one really minds her mood then, because it's a victory for all of us. Warden Wayne has his hands full of Gory's complaints about FR because of it."

"So are you telling me this new director is one of the other officers in the war, one of those you mentioned who is 'in disguise?' "

"Not only that, she's a she! What I mean is, it was quite an upset when Kingline hired a female to direct FR. Anyway, her name is Mavis Isdyche."

"What?"

"It's Jewish-Polish or something like that. Anyway, she's doing a lot of good. She's sidelining Gory and also asserting that women in this company are capable of some of the important work. The deal on those proposals is nothing more than a complicated sob story about poor format, excess material, vague terminology, lost items, etc. But Isdyche has shaped things up. She got to the heart of the matter by telling Kingline's President that she could get the department to save corporate time. Her idea was to put all the proposals together in one place. Isdyche claimed she could do just that, if given 90 days to set up a system for writing the proposals.

"It was a real shake-up. Everyone around here was buzzing

about it. Warden Wayne was fit to be tied and grumpy as hell for three weeks. I don't know all of the in-depth details; Isdyche got here about a month before I did and this is just what I picked up in the lunch-hour gossip. But I guess Isdyche really rattled some teeth down there in that department. Now I hear her staff is the most loyal, stone-solid behind her. The only thing is . . . . a lot of the women won't have anything to do with her because of the rumors."

"I knew there had to be a bug in this success story. What kind of rumors?"

"Gory got so pissed about all this that she attacked the most obvious irrelevant things about Isdyche. So Gory started lesbian-mongering with a passion! No one paid much attention to her because Isdyche isn't in Public Relations, after all. And everyone knew Gory's motives. Plus Isdyche does such a damn good job with FR. I have to admit, though, Isdyche is 'extreme.' She dresses . . . . well, 'masculine.' I've seen a couple of Wayne's memos to her and she's been asked to 'tone down' her personal appearance, but she hasn't. Just ignored the memos, I guess."

"What exactly do you mean when you say she dresses 'masculine?' "

"Well, look for yourself," Jade replied, motioning Berrigan to look across the Kingline Kourt lunch area. With generous stride, Mavis C. Isdyche was tramping the grounds of Kingline, neatly packaged in a woolen tailored suit and black wellington boots, completely engrossed in her own lionization.

"I see what you mean," Berrigan told Jade, nodding in confirmation about Isdyche's appearance. *"She'd be a Pendleton commercial if she was a man."*

Berrigan's Journal — May 3 (copy of a note to Evelyn)
"I'm going to find out about Mavis Isdyche. It must be in that name (Is-dick, Is-ditch, Is-dyke). But is she dyke? I doubt anyone at Kingline knows for sure. Working with her shirt sleeves rolled up like a farmhand and wearing those damn black ankle-boots doesn't add any clarity to the situation. Then there are the tailored suits and ascots, and the fact that she rides a motorcycle to work, even in the snow I'm told. I'm just echoing all the weary stereotypes, I realize.

"While it really isn't that important if Isdyche is a lesbian, or even that I find a lesbian ally in St. Louis, I will say this: Mavis Isdyche is a woman with a will and an obvious independence. She thinks for herself, and that's why I'm going to seek her out.

"And for your humor, Evelyn dear, I am being pursued by a slobbery just-graduated collegiate (not from charm school, unfortunately). Would it be too gauche of me to slug him with my purse?
Love, Berrigan."

Luck provided an opportunity for a meeting between Berrigan and Mavis "Mac" Isdyche. Mr. Johnson asked Berrigan to deliver a package of information to FR so that a proposal could be written for him.

"You do all the mediating, Berrigan. If the FR people have any questions, I'd prefer to send my answers through you. I really don't have time to go down there, and Isdyche is such a pain in the ass anyway."

So! Jade's description of FR's Wonderwoman wasn't unanimously accepted. She might be good at her job, but it was obvious from Mr. Johnson's remark and others Berrigan picked up that Mac was winning no personality contests at Kingline.

Berrigan pondered Mavis Isdyche's ability to offend most of the men at Kingline and Ronald Prince's ability to offend most of the women and decided: *"They ought to give each other a crash course in 'company interaction!' "*

Heading for the door marked "Film Requisition: Mavis C. Isdyche, Director," Berrigan wondered, *(Like walking into the lion's maw? Well, here goes.)* As she reached for the doorknob, a wolf-whistle from down the hall distracted her. Turning, she saw Ronald Prince wave, then disappear up the stairs, tapping his well-shined wingtips like a schoolboy.

The central office area of FR was buzzing with activity: three Xerox machines were grinding out copies with assorted beeps and squawks, four or five women were filing and chattering, popping their gum excitedly. Two assistants were on the phone, and another phone in a side office rang constantly. That was Mac's office. She was rarely in it because she spent most of her time as ringleader out in the Central Area.

"Now goddamn it, Carole, I told you not to release that stuff back to Wayne without making those changes! Didn't I tell you that, Carole? We've wasted three days, and these films are top priority! They're *good* for a change, for chrissakes! Now get after it!"

The voice began booming from the back of the Central Area, emerging in person from behind three rows of ceiling-high filing cabinets. In all the activity, no one had noticed Berrigan until Isdyche looked up from her conversation with Carole. She saw the manila folder Berrigan was holding.

"Tell me," she said, looking Berrigan squarely in the face. Berrigan wasn't sure what to answer or if she was actually being addressed.

"Tell me!" Isdyche persisted. Berrigan finally awakened from her fascination with the frenetic pace of this den of mystery, FR.

"Oh! I have some information for a proposal, for Mr. Johnson."

Isdyche turned and barked to a bespectacled woman with long stringy hair, sitting at one of the back desks.

"Miller! You've got a customer up here. How many times do I have to tell you to pay attention!"

"Sorry, sorry, Mac," she mumbled, scurrying up to the counter to take the folder.

75

"*Guess you just can't get good help these days?*" Berrigan offered as a joke, a throw-away to make conversation.

Isdyche leveled her. "Until you work down here, you're not qualified to judge. If anyone here is incompetent, it's from overwork."

Then she exited into her office briskly, where she ignored the nagging phone, belching out yet another order to anyone in earshot: "Get on that switchboard operator up there! I don't have time to answer this damn phone!"

Berrigan observed the brute loyalty Mavis Isdyche inspired, and the undeniable observable reality that the department was swamped. Despite the fact that Warden Wayne would surely not find FR a "well spiffed" department, news traveled in lauditory terms about the ability of the FR staff to turn out most projects on time. The sour grapes people claimed there just wasn't time to change FR's presentations, and some said the men were afraid to cross Mac. Berrigan had formed no definite opinions about FR, Mavis Isdyche, or the gossipy reactions to her department. She was intrigued, but as yet uncommitted.

Several days after her visit to Isdyche's madhouse, she had an opportunity to decisively ally herself with the infamous FR director. Walking through the Kingline Kourt, Berrigan overheard a malicious indictment of Isdyche, coming from a group of secretaries on their lunch-hour. One of the younger women from the typing pool was doing a dance, singing to the tune of "Mac the Knife," but she had changed the words and was singing "Mac the Dyke."

> "Oh the dyke, babe,
> Has such eyes, dear
> And she casts them
> On your boobs!"

Her audience broke into giggles and some one of them chimed in, "God, is she ever weird!"

"Do you think she's really queer?" another asked.

"How could she *not* be! I mean, she's a *boss,* and those boots!"

"You know that motorcycle parked out in the lot? It's hers! I wouldn't work down there in FR for anything. She probably pats all those girls on the butt!"

"No, no," one of the group offered wisely, "lezzies don't do that. They nudge you up against the file cabinets!"

Disgusted, Berrigan didn't wait to hear any more. In their criticism of Mavis Isdyche, these women were as much stereotypes as Mac herself, right in the mold of the vicious, self-serving bitches they often enacted: Woman as Gossip-Harpie, or what Berrigan called "*sharp-nosed girls.*"

(Jealous. All of them are jealous, because Mac expresses herself. She's her own person, and they're afraid of her independence. It shows them their own cages.)

76

In this contemplation, Berrigan turned the corner, spotting Isdyche alone on one of the benches. Mac didn't look up; she was reading. Berrigan made out the title of the book: *Lesbian Politics.*
(No better time to approach than the present, I guess.)
"Thinking of running for Congress?"
Isdyche looked up then, but did not close the book or attempt to hide the cover. "Not really. Vice President, maybe."
"Will that be on the lavender ticket?"
"Only if I can be assured of a large Violet Groupie sector. I'll need all the fans I can get."
"Yes, I understand they tend to be a fickle group."
"Not the ones I know."
Isdyche knew the conversation was traveling on two levels. Her caution was evident.
"Then you're most fortunate, Ms. Isdyche. Especially if your followers are, shall we say, willing to let their ideals 'out of the closet,' publicly. Whatever strain of politics people are into these days, they all need a good shot of honesty and sincerity."
"So who would you recommend in politics. Who gets your vote?"
Berrigan now had an opportunity to return to Mavis Isdyche the same unhesitating direct approach the FR director had extended her on their first meeting.
"My vote goes to Sappho."
Mac's unflinching gaze did not waver.
"Because we haven't had a poet as president yet."
Berrigan had made a point with Mavis Isdyche, although response to the conversation in the Kingline Kourt wasn't immediate. Berrigan didn't press contact for several days. Finally, she had to relay more information on Johnson's proposal.
This time, Miller jumped up from her desk at the back and hurried to the counter, having taken the first reprimand from Mac seriously. "Can I help you?" she chirped, and dispensed with Berrigan's materials quickly. As she was shuffling the new additions to the proposal off to one side of numerous stacks, Isdyche rounded the cabinets, just as she had the first time Berrigan visited FR.
When Mac saw Berrigan, she didn't hesitate. " "Step into my office, please." Miller hustled off to her own desk, and Berrigan entered the side office. Closing the door behind them, Isdyche exhibited her notorious brevity.
"I won't waste time mincing words or waiting on quizzical glances across the Kourt and Kingline's crowded rooms. I gathered from our conversation the other day that if you're not a full-fledged gay sister, you're surely a sympathizer. Most of the women I know would have balked noticeably at seeing the cover of *Lesbian Politics,* and most of the women I know don't read Sappho just for variety from Emily Dickinson.
"If I'm way off-base, you can tell me to go to hell and we'll

forget it. And if you say anything to anyone, that won't matter either because everyone around here has already neatly filed me away as a roaring dyke. But I've been looking for someone ever since I got to St. Louis, just for some intelligent conversation. This place is running me up the wall! If you're interested, I can take you to some places here, several good bars. Let me know at your convenience. That's all."

A well-timed phone call interrupted Berrigan's response and she left the office with a non-commital, *"I'll get back to you."*

Leaving this unexpected exchange with Mac, Berrigan bumped into the Prince of Prurience himself, Ronald Rapacious. She fairly stumbled into his arms, to his delight.

"At last! Your resistance fails! Come away with me to the darkroom!"

Berrigan pushed away from him and headed towards the elevator, Ronald following undaunted.

"How about dinner with me tonight?"

"No thanks."

"Busy?"

"Uh huh."

"Tomorrow? What about dinner tomorrow?"

"Nope."

"Next Thursday?"

"Sorry."

"April 3rd of next year?"

The elevator door opened; Berrigan stepped inside and then she and Ronald were facing each other.

"We could go to the Opera."

Berrigan shook her head.

"A rock concert? A karate match? A war-movie?"

The door shut again on Ronald's persistence, and his suggestions echoed up the elevator shaft.

"A circus? Amusement park? Dog race? Cock fight?"

Berrigan's Journal – May 10

Sometimes my karma is too easy; the way it unfolds is too predictable. I begin to distrust the Fates. There must be a reason I went up to Isdyche and spoke so freely. She's certainly formidable. But I do tend to over-analyze myself. So enough! As for her offer of the bars . . . I'm hesitant. I doubt they would be the answer to my loneliness. But I've indulged long enough in my self-pitying solitude, endless days in the apartment watching the seasons mellow the street walkers on Foxglove. This is no solution either.

Evelyn's letters have helped a great deal; her writing always makes me laugh. But even her loyal support loses something when translated long distance.

I must be fair to myself and not ignore what seems to be yawning wide open to me. And I do need a friend here. I know I should trust my perceptions and impressions. I don't think a friendship with Mac or exploring the St. Louis bars will do me harm. After all, I have lived past the crystal penguin.

Had a dream about Syru last night . . . . we were making love and she dissolved out of my arms into a newspaper photograph under the headline: "Women's Libber Jailed for Leading March."

Berrigan's Journal — May 11

I called Mac with an invitation to supper at my apartment. She'll be the first visitor in my St. Louis home! She accepted, and we decided on Thursday evening at 7:00. I'm not nervous about her visit, except I do wonder what Jade will ask me if she finds out!

What I really wish for is Evelyn's helping hand with the spaghetti; she has more of an Italian aesthetic than I do! At least I don't have to bring the wine. That will be Mac's contribution.

(I was so excited I sent a note to Evelyn about this without postage!)

Berrigan's Journal — May 13

3:30 A.M. — the hour's late, but I'm wide awake, even knowing that I have to go to work in just a few hours. But I want to get some of my impressions down about tonight's dinner guest. This entry might be entitled: "Guess Who Came to Dinner: Mavis C. Isdyche."

In a word, she *surprises*. Mavis Isdyche isn't just the austere motorcycle mama barking blustery orders on Kingline terrain. There is a lot more to her, as there always is to any woman (Even Gory!).

Seated on the floor of my little attic pad, Mac grew comfortable, her personality aging with the wine and spaghetti (nearly as good as Evelyn's). First we talked around specifics; then we talked about our backgrounds. I found the whole of my time with Syru winding out of me, unstoppable. It's been bottled in tighter than I thought. But Mac's a very good listener, which surprised me most of all. Her usual pace is so hell-bent, I figured she'd never stop to hear anyone else.

I found out Mac comes from New York and some sordid scenes which partially explain her need to always charge at the world from behind a thick wall of self-absorbed bravado.

Growing up poor in New York, her allies weren't soft, and her femaleness was no protection from the everyday violence. Having held up a service station at gunpoint when she was 15, and been "fucked over, roughed up, and finally abandoned" by too many boyfriends, Mac told me she left New York "to escape the whirlpool of violence — it sucks you in, without allowance for innocent bystanders."

On to Chicago, where she worked for a custom tailor for affluent men and took night classes to finish a college degree in media. There she fell into a "fag set" via some of her employer's most elite customers.

"I guess the pretty boys in Chicago saw a strength in me missing in so many of their own friends. Maybe they just thought I'd make a good bouncer. In any case, I spent most of my time in the men's bars or at exclusive apartment parties for Chicago gays. I began to meet some of the women, most of them arty, on drugs, some of them swinging gay with their husbands.

"I scouted out information on the women's bars and gradually started spending my time there. Eventually I made many friends in Chicago, got into several scrapes, but it was good experience.

"I didn't have much opportunity to advance with the tailor, though, so when I got a line on the Kingline job, having my college work finally finished, I went for it. I couldn't believe it when I actually got the job!"

After Mac's description of her life, I told her my own limited experience with gay bars. I've only been in one and that was just for a few minutes. She said if I wanted to go out, she'd be my escort, so we made a date for Saturday night. I wish Evelyn were here; she'd love this new adventure!

Berrigan's Journal — June 14

In these weeks since I last wrote in the journal, I've spent almost every night out in the bars with Mac, observing the ebb and flow of personalities in what I can only call "The Big Melodrama." These are a new breed of women: pool players, beer chuggers, pin-ball wizards, with a language all their own.

The most popular bar in St. Louis is "The Salon," where Mac and I went that first Saturday night. I quickly learned why "The Salon" is so well attended. It features go-go dancers wearing only lavender g-strings and pasties to cover their honor.

After my eyes adjusted to the dim light, I located the audience focal point: a stage under a black light at the far end of the bar, upon which a shapely lady was undulating to the latest Top Hit jungle beat.

"That's Sharon, Queen of the Dancers," Mac told me. "She's femme."

(Femme. *Strange . . . . we start with labels and end up with labels, like numbers around our necks.*)

We found a table off to one side of the stage, and Mac pointed out and named some of the bar regulars.

K.J. — The bartender: tall and glistening, a throwback to the
   Amazon era of blonde, hard-breasted women.
Stager — She can spot a vulnerability and score on it, instantly making enemies or lovers, all of them victims.
Trucker — Women love her for her hardness, her distance, and
   because she rejects them with style.
Cowboy — With a heart of gold, a faded neckscarf, and boots
   dusty from waiting so long to be abandoned at a lover's
   bedside.

Teddy — Pimping with Annie, spaced on heroin, she is empty womanflesh.

Annie — She stepped out of the gun-moll days. Of Teddy she says: "I know she's bad, but what can I say? I love her. She's my Big Mamma."

The Pearl — "If Mae West had a sistah, ah'd be her!" You find The Pearl launched against the bar, in a dress like a black limousine, her hair polished with light and ivory combs, her eyes full of white coal: she's *that* hot. I've never seen it, but Mac says she carries a stiletto in that black dress. She lets a few women love her, but they pay for the privilege.

There are more, an endless parade: 200-pound Indian women who nearly pow-wow'ed the place into a shambles; the glitter set who stare out of an acid fog and wobble on eight-inch platform shoes; the femmes with yearning wet eyes; the butches muscling in competition to win love without admitting the need for it; the fighters and screamy squabblers.

By the end of the first evening I'd had too much drinking and dancing to know what was going on, or to notice that Sharon had been watching me during her breaks. When Mac left our table to go to the bar for another drink, Sharon approached me and said, "You're new out, I hear. Are you with Mac now?"

"We're friends. Just friends. I like your dancing."

I couldn't help noticing that Sharon had put on a shorty robe to cover the few strands of her dancing costume.

"You like my dancing enough to come home with me, and let me be your Big W.?"

I didn't understand what she meant by the remark exactly; I hadn't savvied all the lingo and the bar games yet. All I could think of was what Mac told me when we first walked in, and so it was the first thing that came out of my mouth.

"But you're femme, aren't you?"

The inanity of what I said came from being drunk and naive, but Sharon was unsympathetic. My remark sealed my doom with the Queen of the Dancers, who figured her offer was good enough for any woman. From then on, she called me "Mac's Bitch." Every time we go to "The Salon," she tries to make trouble for me, or at least get close enough to me to deliver a "drop-dead" epithet.

There are two other bars in St. Louis, but the crowd I've described usually revolves in all three. At "The Blade," the leather-jacketed toughs hang out, giving it an aura of s-and-m that glowers, heavy as incense.

The third bar, "La Focha," was small and hazy when Mac and I visited. With the noise of the telephone, jukebox, and pinball machine in competition, we couldn't hear each other talk, so we didn't stay long. As we were leaving, I noticed a woman in the bathroom doorway. She was in a nod, her head at rest against the toilet seat.

Even after this short time out in the bars, I know they can never become a sanctuary for me. Mac enjoys the excitement and variety, the adventure of women-in-transit, the spontenaity. But to me, it's a shallow hearth these sisters huddle by, absent of warmth. They play emotional roulette, escaping themselves between musical bedsheets, changing partners as casually as underwear. Drinking, dancing, going home alone in the cold blue night, or to dry fucking with strangers: this is desolation, worse than any I saw in the faces on the streets, the faces of those Doris told me I could not save. And the loneliness of the bars is worse than my own lonely bed.

At first I bought the idea that gay people come to these places to be together because there's no other meeting place. But I'm not convinced, because there is no "community" atmosphere. We're more like shipwrecked victims cast on common shore. We stare at one another, drenched to the bone with criticism. Wary and jerking with insecurities, we are unable to gauge the perils in one another. So we drink and dance, until the perils and the criticism disappear.

We . . . . I must count myself in this bar syndrome; night after night, I've been watching a vicious circle of trivial jealousies, endless treachery, a kind of life "on the make" that never relents. I will not deny that I have been and am lonely, and Mac is good company. But we are not lovers, nor "butch buddies." We're just the more sturdy victims of the shipwreck; less myopic, but still victims.

Where are the carefree girls laughing in the loft? I would rather be with them there now, or lost under the spell of Dulcea reading Woolf's Lady Orlando. I would rather be drinking beer with Evelyn.

But back to some specifics . . . . Stager has been at me incessantly, since my first appearance out with Mac. Her well-disguised interest in me is a means for locating my "soft spot." She knows I'm green and never misses an opportunity to capitalize on that. Her favorite trick is to send drinks from me (without my knowledge) to the diesel-dykes in the bar, knowing full well these women will want to find me to offer a personal thank-you. It's embarrassing and dehumanizing to have to tell a bulging-eyed desperate mammoth that I just can't go home with her. Mac calls them "stompers" and says for my own survival, I should ignore them or be rude.

But maybe we all have the same potential karma that would make us huge, misshapen, desperate mammoths. I can't solve the dilemma of how to deal with these women, or Stager's manipulation of them in regard to me.

Almost every night, Cowboy will be leaning in a corner of the bar, one boot up against the wall. She'll watch the women dance, sip her beer with slow philosophy, occasionally looking at The Pearl, as if for all the world her happiness could be made by the approval of the stiletto-lady. I've talked to Cowboy a few times; she's reserved, uncertain, gun-shy, like all of us at one time or another. She's needy for the special companion another woman can be. When she gets drunk, Cowboy bursts into wavering rendition of "Home on the Range," until someone pulls her off the bar and takes her home.

Teddy and Annie wobble in late, in a flurry of fur and the glint off Teddy's silver cane. She admits she's pretentious to carry the cane, "But when the bottles fly, it's nice to have next to me."

They pass from table to table, oohing and ahhing with friends, hugging, flirting. So many of the women they know have borrowed money from Teddy, or stolen an hour's worth of Annie, or found a fix with Teddy when no one else in the city had a pinch. Their cordiality is insurance for the next time they need something.

After an hour or so these two rise and wobble out again, Teddy heavy against Annie. "We showed, babe," Teddy will say, "we always show. Like clockwork. They need our class, you know. We're the only flash in town."

But of all the characters who fade in and out of the black-light reflections of "The Salon," Trucker is my favorite woman. She's a no muss personality, without an easy key: effusive with silence, vastly private, relentlessly unsolveable.

There are no excuses or explanations for Trucker's women. She's an indiscriminate collector, with a gamut of lovelies always willing and ready: models, stewardesses, hookers, ex-Vegas dancers, guru students with flowered hair, anonymous brunette nurses. None of them have any longevity because Trucker's ultimate position is "untouchable." She enjoys conquest but refuses commitment. I think she fears familiarity. It might make her predictable.

But I guess I pose no threat, must seem in fact like spongecake to her. Especially after what happened two weeks ago, which made us special friends.

I had seen her writing on a napkin and discovered that she was jotting poetry. When she caught me reading what she'd written, she was angry. Later, she burst into my bathroom stall and started pushing and pulling me, shaking me like I was a bad child. We fell out of the door and onto the feet of others waiting to get a free stall, Rather than a real wrestling match, our jostling was more her way of proving to me that she wasn't weak for writing poetry.

I knew that without the gymnastics, of course, but she wasn't sure and didn't ask me directly (a typical bar game). When we were finally retrieved from underfoot by Mac and Stager as unofficial bouncers, they didn't understand our laughter in light of the badly wrenched stall door and the ruckus we'd made. Too used to the screaming blowouts of quarreling lovers, they were surprised when we didn't come up swinging. Trucker may be the only true "sister" I make on this tour.

Huddles of dancers, arms locked loving, kissing, laughing, hands caressing waists, breasts, shoulders, long passionate kisses everywhere: my eyes are full of what women do in the bar.

Then a white-bulb alarm flashes: one time, two times. These huddles of dancers just finishing touches and sorting partners become busted blots of bodies, seated, drinking, distinctly apart and untouching.

Sergeants Caine and Blocker, with their Captain Foil, forge into the cavern of the bar with rude flashlights and clinking handcuffs.

"I.D., please . . . . bitch," one of them mumbles. The Blue Boys and their Leader each have night sticks, brandished, hard, on hand. "Just in case, just in case." They bang their boots on the floor, stomping past each booth, looking grossly into every face, hoping openly for a hint, even a hint of trouble. But nothing comes.

Caine asks me, "What's a nice girl like you doing in a place like this?"

"Gee officer, I got lost on the way to 7-11." He does not think I'm funny. "Some lez comedienne," he mumbles. I do not think he is funny.

Finally they all swagger away, clinking and bristling with disdain, these he-men with badges, on the loose. In the flash of their revolving red light as they leave, they gruffly sneer, mostly hoping: "We scared those dykes shitless."

Inside the bar, the bodies, women-bodies in the dark whispering, laughing, brush billfolds back into pockets and grow together again in huddles, for more caressing, dancing, breathing kisses, hoping but mostly knowing: "We scared those pigs shitless."

Berrigan's Journal — June 24

All I saw was a flurry of fists. Someone yelled, "You don't love her, you sonofabitch!" More yelling: "Cunt! Whore!" And then a table went over, glasses shattering as the melee spilled onto our laps.

"Get out, get out of this bar!" An angry bouncer shoved a woman out of the door, obscenities spitting from their angry mouths. Yelling again, then sobbing: we were all quiet, watching, with our fear in our laps glinting like blood on the chips of glass.

My guts were grinding when the fists started flashing. It is so terrifying when women fight.

Berrigan's Journal — June 26

Phone rang at 4 A.M., just as I was on the verge of exhausted sleep. It was Ronald Prince. He wanted to know if I was dreaming about him!

* * * * * *

What will six weeks of bar-hopping do for the energy level of a

Kingline secretary? Assuredly leave her often hung-over, sluggish, inattentive, careless, and the object of administrative consternation!

During Berrigan's odyssey out into the world of St. Louis gay bardom, her work at Kingline suffered. As a result, she was called into Mr. Johnson's office. After he painstakingly reiterated to Berrigan that he must exact some standards from her since she was the secretary and he was the executive, she explained to him that being in St. Louis alone, her blooming social life had gotten the best of her. She said she would get herself back on a more sane schedule so that careless errors in her work would be avoided.

"It's certainly understandable," Mr. Johnson commented, taking Berrigan's story at face value. "An attractive single woman in St. Louis . . . . yes I *certainly* understand your dilemma. The pleasures of excess overtake even the best of us at times. However, I trust that you'll adjust so you can handle your duties here at work equally well. But 'keep up the good work,' if you know what I mean!"

And with a wink, the inquisition was over, with Berrigan still in good standing with her Associate Producer. It seemed that her job failures could be tolerated by Mr. Johnson, on his assumption that it was for a cause even more relevant than Company Time: Good Ole American Copulation!

Unfortunately, Berrigan's preoccupation had not dimmed the glow of Ronald Prince's perseverance. She found a box of mushy chocolates on her desk and a vase of roses, with a note from the Prince:

"Wasn't it Shakespeare who advised wooing a woman with sweets and a bouquet? If his technique doesn't work, then I'll try another way!"

Meanwhile, back at the Kingline Kourt, Jade had asked Berrigan to lunch several times, but Mac always seemed to get the drop on her time first. Finally, Jade caught Berrigan in the supply room and asked why Isdyche was suddenly so interested in a friendship.

"Do you think she's after your bod?" Jade asked.

"I hope not. I'm no match for those motorcycle boots!"

"No, really, Berrigan. What's she like?"

"Interesting . . . . not the berserk lesbian man-hater everyone thinks she is. That's just a work image, and an effective one at that! Maybe that's the real reason everyone around here has it in for her. Their own flack doesn't work as well warding off Wayne and his bitchy memos!"

"Yeah, well, we all need to develop some kind of camouflage around here, some kind of smoke-screen. Otherwise we'd go crazy! But don't stay so out of touch with me for too long, lady! And keep me posted. We underground warriors have to stick together!"

Jade's allegiance didn't stray from Berrigan, despite her new

affiliation with Mac. Jade was not scared off from friendship by
rumors or idle gossip. However, before she could become a more
supportive ally, she left Kingline unexpectedly. Berrigan later
received a postcard from Rio from Jade, who had met a revivalist
belly dancer and joined his traveling troop dancing and evangeliz-
ing.

Berrigan's Journal — June 28
     Work was the pits today and I dragged home achey and out of
sorts. No cat nor martini nor roommate to comfort me. But my day
was made by a blessing in my mailbox: a letter from Evelyn!
     I've sent her some of my journal pages, describing the bars.
She wrote back telling me to be careful but also commenting on the
vividness of my description. She says she thinks she saw a double
for The Pearl in a singles bar in Hartford!
     She went home to see her family during a break in summer
classes. Nothing is changed except they weren't thrilled about her
announcing she wants to move again, out of the sorority house.
     "I could have used the excuse that it's full of lesbians," she
writes, "but I didn't on your account. Ain't I liberal!"
     In the final paragraph of her letter, she mentions the glimmer
of a promising affair, but won't "name names." I've got to write her
back right away and see what (or who) she's up to!

Berrigan's Journal — June 30
     Mac called; there's a Drag Revue on at "The Salon." But I
decided to stay home and write my parents an over-due letter so
they won't have the Connecticut National Guard out looking for
their long-lost daughter!

Berrigan's Journal — July 2
     I'm reminiscing as the Independence Day weekend comes up
about how I used to spend the Fourth of July with my family. Dad
and I would sometimes go to the country, somewhere out in the
trees. Then we'd set off fire crackers, both of us whooping like crazy
kids, blowing up dirt piles and sending cans jumping in the air.
     Mom would sit in the car until we were done, having patiently
endured our "ya-hoos!" coming from within the trees. We'd picnic
and everything tasted so good. My mother's face would get pink
with the sun. None of us were worrying about my growing up then.
     Again Mac calls, entreating me to come out with her for the
party at "The Salon." My first inclination is to say no and go to the
pet shop instead to buy myself a friendly cat. (Something about
that isn't right either — it feels like permanence.) But Mac
wouldn't understand if I tried to explain so I agree to go.
     My contact with Mac has been strained lately. Every time I
start to talk about anything besides our pool scores, she changes

the subject. She knows I don't find in the bars what she does but she won't listen to any of the ideas that interest me. Heaven forbid we should discuss Lib! Occasionally I can get her to talk about Kingline. I've spouted some of my theories about corporate oppression and executive woman-hating, and she just says, "Come on, Berrigan. None of those executives are that smart. Besides, if they hate women, why are they always lookin' for a lay?"

I guess Syru spoiled me, as did the NAW women. Even though my life in Bingham became intolerable, at least for that time I had friends who were exploring the same spaces I was. I miss them now, even whiney Alice.

Berrigan's Journal — July 7

The bars have become a great charade I can no longer entertain. There just isn't anything there for me. I'm bored, restless, even scared sometimes by what I see there. Especially after what happened on the Fourth.

Mac and I were having a fairly good time, dancing with lit sparklers under the black-light at "The Salon." A comedy revue from one of the gay groups in Chicago performed and the local women's band played.

Mid-evening, Stager came up to me, leading a kinky-wigged teeny-bopper by the hand. The girl was stoned and stumbling. When I saw the two of them coming towards me, I tried to move but Stager preguessed me and blocked my way.

"Here," she said, giving me the girl's hand. "Take her. I'm done." And then she disappeared into the crowd of dancers, leaving the girl leaning heavily against me.

"I sure need a j. Oh god, do I need a good j," she kept saying to me. "You got any grass, huh?"

I managed to find out her address, and put her in a cab home. I didn't see Stager again until about midnight, when she asked me to dance with her. She was drunk and a little stumbly.

After I refused to dance with her several times, I finally agreed. But I decided not to ignore her rudeness earlier in the evening.

"Look Stager, I'm not fond of anyone who regards their date as 'leftovers.' What you did was a cheap trick."

"Come on, Berrigan. It was just a joke! That chick didn't even hear what I said. She didn't even know who she was with!"

"Stop trying to sham me. I'm not green anymore."

"Okay, okay, I'm sorry. Come outside with me for a minute and let's talk where it's quieter."

"Just let me get my escort. She knows karate."

"Come on! I just wanna *talk!*"

Stager sounded sincere, enough to make me abandon all the survival tactics Mac had been trying to teach me. I decided to go with her since Mac was busy doing a revival of the jitterbug. We stepped out the back door. Stager walked a ways from the door, following the wall of the building with her hand to steady herself. The air was cool and refreshing after all the heat and smoke in the bar.

"You seen my fuckin' cigarettes? I can't find nothin' out here; it's too dark. You seen my fuckin' cigarettes?"

"You need to walk around out here in the air, I think."

Stager found her cigarettes and lit one; it's red tip shone in the dark.

"Hey. How come I never see you with anyone? How come you're only with Mac? She's not your lover so how come she's the only woman I see you with? You want yourself a honey?" She took a wobbly step towards me.

"When I find a honey, then I'll have one, I guess."

Stager laughed, spitting out her just-lit cigarette. "Look no more then! Your honey is here!"

She tried to move quickly towards me and tripped on several boxes stacked by the building. As I caught her falling, she trapped me underneath her, garbage cans clanging as we fell into them. She was still laughing, and trying to kiss me. I couldn't move and got angry.

"Get the hell off me!" I yelled. Stager got surly, pushing on me roughly. "Think you're so wise to me now?" she growled. I could smell the beer on her breath and feel how hot and heavy she was.

At that moment, a can lid came down on Stager like a cymbal of vengeance and she melted away from me, replaced by Trucker's face.

"You okay, kid?" she said, helping me up. I didn't even thank her. I just headed for home.

By the time I got home I was shaking, angry and scared. I called Evelyn a couple of times and finally got an answer. She managed to calm me down and console me.

"Can't take that 'hangin' out with toughs' jazz, huh?" she teased when I felt stronger. "Better come on home, Berrigan. I sure miss you."

When we hung up, I realized how much I missed her too. My head has been in a fog — full of empty thoughts about Syru, the bars, Kingline. Evelyn reminded me that there are some good things about Bingham.

I went back to "The Salon" on the 5th to find Trucker. She wasn't there yet when I arrived so I talked to K.J. She didn't have much to say, just smiled a lot. She's beautiful but transparent, this bar Adonis, like the pretended love I see here. Finally I stopped making inane small talk and just sat, looking at the shattered crystals in my ice cubes and staring at the rows of liquor bottles with their pink pour-spouts looking like so many wilted forlorn penises, garishly out of place in a lesbian bar.

When Trucker finally came in, she told me she'd found out that the incident with Stager was a set-up. She was trying to settle a score for Sharon, the dancer I'd offended my first night out in St. Louis.

When I asked Trucker why she helped me out, she retreated into herself, unable to decide whether to be shy or aloof.

"Rolling a chick in the alley is cheap. Stager has no style. She gives the bar a bad name."

When I questioned Trucker further, she admitted that since I had kept quiet about her writing poetry, she figured I was okay.

"Besides, it occurred to me a long time ago that you might get into trouble with one of these bad eggs. The possibility of a reward for saving you was very appealing."

I couldn't help laughing at Trucker's confession. She was embarrassed, the "untouchable" finally coming within reach of someone, so I thought the laughter might save her. And what she told me, revealing so much of herself, brought me close to tears so the laughter saved me too.

* * * * * *

Despite Trucker's unique timing in solving Berrigan's conflict with Stager, another one was brewing with Mac.

After a phone call from Mac that sounded urgent, they met in the same spot on the Kingline Kourt where Berrigan had first seen Mac reading *Lesbian Politics*. They hadn't talked since the Fourth but Berrigan knew Mac had heard the story about Stager through the grapevine.

"What's up? You sounded worried over the phone."

"I'm not worried. I'm pissed. Royally pissed. You made me look like a damned fool last weekend. You didn't even come to me for help, you just split."

"Mac, I'm tired of all the bar games. They don't interest me anymore. Maybe they never did."

"Don't play Nancy Noble with me and start in with your theories about the bars and your theories on a 'greater concept of women,' for chrissakes!"

"It's pretty simple. There's nothing in the bars for me. The kind of women I want to meet aren't there. The kind of life I want to live isn't there."

"Now tell me the answer is 'sisterhood,' and prove it by showing me all the sisters you've made here at Kingline!"

"Can you disprove it? If the bars are such a good deal, where's your lover? Those bars aren't the stomping grounds of lovers. They belong solely to escapists . . . . some of them in tailored suits."

"Look who's talking! You're ridiculous, Berrigan, living your life kneeling at a shrine to Sappho, reciting prayers for the Second Coming, the Amazon Rebirth. What a fool, what a bad joke you are! And you don't even know it!

"You're telling me *I'm* out of touch with reality! Everyone has a right to make their own choices, with those women at the bars, me included, as no exception. They don't get on any soapboxes and preach any sermons. They don't think their way is the only one that exists. I'm sure that's why you don't fit in!"

"Okay, Mac. This is your reality but not mine. I accept that. Can't you? I'm not trying to convert you. You never gave me a chance! I thought I could find something by running away from my past troubles. I was wrong. But the bars aren't solution either. So you aren't going to become a feminist and I'm not gonna become a regular at 'The Salon.' But that doesn't mean we have to be enemies. You were my first friend when I came to St. Louis. That has to count for something."

Berrigan's allusion to their first night of magic and friendship took the sting out of the argument. They reached a temporary halt to hostility.

"Libbers will be libbers, I guess," Mac concluded.

"Once a pool jockey, always a pool jockey. You can't kid me. I'm not green anymore."

Though they parted in peace, Berrigan knew they had not resolved their differences about the bar and Mac would continue her social life there. Berrigan decided not to waste any more time being lonely and confused. She made plans to head back to Bingham and Evelyn, even though there were no clear answers in her thoughts about what lay past returning home. She sent Evelyn a telegram.

"I need a sympatica. Will be there in ten days. Get out my army cot; be on your doorstep soon.
Love Berrigan."

Mac took the news without surprise, but she held no grudge about their argument.

"I don't guess you want to go to 'The Salon' for 'one for the road'?"

"No thanks."

"You hitching?"

"Yeah."

"The least I can do is chauffeur you to the highway on my Harley."

"Now that's an offer I won't refuse!"

Mr. Johnson took the news of Berrigan's leaving in stride when she announced it to him.

"I'll be here until Friday," she told him. He winked back, "Some lucky fella, eh?"

(Sorry, it's not Ronald Prince, much as you'd like to get rid of him.)

On Wednesday, Mr. Johnson had carnations delivered to Berrigan's desk, with a card attached saying, "So long and happy hunting!" An interoffice memo from Ronald Prince beckoned, "Are you sure you don't want to reconsider? Do you really know what you're missing? This is your last chance to meet me in the darkroom."

At ten minutes to five on Friday, Berrigan was putting the cover on her IBM witmaster, clearing her desk and collecting her things to leave everything well-spiffed when she heard the sound of nuts rattling in a can. Turning, Berrigan found Gory at her desk, offering her a present: cashews wrapped in a yellow bow.

"I heard cashews were your favorites. Maybe you can eat them on the road to wherever you're going. It's a good thing you're getting out of here while you still have a chance to go after what you really want."

"Don't you have what you want, Alma?"

"All I ever wanted was a nagging husband and a couple of grimy kids. What have I ended up with? Fake furs, twelve useless years here, and an impotent poodle. Certainly your future will be brighter."

She squeezed Berrigan's arm and walked back to her desk.

On her way to meet Mac, Berrigan passed the door to the typing pool and thought of the thousands of Kingline letters finished at the bottom with the executives' initials in All Caps and the typists' in small letters. She flushed, angry with the madness of secretaries chained to typewriters, destined to spend their careers as "small letters," inconsequential, insignificant. It was too much.

She walked to the Kingline coffee room and scrawled a note, which she left as her legacy to the Kingline Korporate Kaptains. She taped it to the coffee urn. At the door she thought fleetingly of Syru and smiled, looking back at the note.

"From all of us secretaries to all of you executives: Cram this coffeepot up your corporate ass.
Berrigan."

CHAPTER 6

Cars and trucks and dingy diners: three days on the road left Berrigan weary, exhausted from long waits in the sun for a ride. Travel by hitch-hiking was cheap but hard: miles and miles fending off the rude suggestions of horny truck drivers or riding with lonely women who droned in monotone about their neglectful husbands. Sometimes Berrigan gave way to the hypnosis of the blaring radios and the endless zips of yellow highway stripes. She daydreamed as the highway was eaten up by the cars in huge flat slabs. Finally in Pittsburgh on the fourth day, she considered either taking a bus on into Bingham or calling Evelyn. But she knew Evelyn had little time for an unexpected trip, and Berrigan could afford a bus ticket.

As she was turning to walk off the highway and back towards a diner to call the closest bus line, a bright red Ambassador passed her and then scuttled to a stop in the summer dust. A young woman called out the driver-side window: "Hey, come on! Wanna ride?"

Berrigan went up to the car.

"Hi, I'm Corette Hill," the driver offered. "I'm going to my mother's place in Vermont, by way of a stop in Connecticut. Can I give you a lift in that direction?"

The days on the road left Berrigan little energy for cheery friendliness. The truck drivers had taken their toll on her patience, so her attitude was dry and to the point.

"Where in Connecticut?"

"New London."

"I can get off at the state line and be almost home."

"Good! I'll enjoy the company."

Berrigan climbed into the Ambassador, depositing her backpack and suitcase in the back seat.

"Careful," Corette told her, "don't lean anything on my canvasses."

"Are you an artist?"

"Well, I've been painting for about five years. And doing some sculpture. Now my mother is the *real* artist in the family! She was at her easel right up to the time of my delivery! I wish I could paint like she does."

Corette fired up the car and they pulled back onto the highway.

"We're now hitting 48 miles per hour, which must be a record

92

for this car! This is a speed I call 'high putter.' Our driving time won't be very fast, I'm afraid. But hey! You haven't told me your name."

"Berrigan. I'm going to Bingham."

"I've heard of the college there. Are you in school?"

"I was at one time, but luckily no more."

"Did you graduate?"

"In a way. Say, New London is a sort of a funny place to visit. Or are you going into the Navy?"

Corette laughed with a resilience that blew away some of the dust seeping into Berrigan's good humor.

"I'd never make a good sailor: all that saluting and uniform pressing seems like a waste of time to me. I guess regimentation wasn't part of my upbringing."

"Then do you live in New London?"

"No. You see, a friend of mine is there to be inducted into the Navy, but he's having a problem. It's rather . . . ah . . . hard to explain. It's a touchy situation."

"I'm not trying to pry."

"Well actually, I think it's a funny story if you've got a liberal sense of humor."

"Try me."

"My friend's name is Billy Acorn. His mother was a Jamaican stick of ebony and his father a fiery red swig of Irish whiskey, which makes Billy one of the few black dudes in the world with naturally red hair! Besides being a hybrid, Billy thinks he's the world's slickest jive-talker, and he's always trying to prove it. Unfortunately, his con artist talents are dubious, so he's been in a number of snags that have been real doozies! Believe me, I know because I've always bailed him out! But to make the story short, Billy is a sometimes performer — a female impersonator, known as 'Shamrock Sally' in our stomping grounds, which is Charleston.

"But anyway, Billy and the most recent of his many lovers had a big fight. In a rash moment, he decided to join the Navy. But what Billy didn't realize, which is not unusual for him, is that signing enlistment papers is no joke. Uncle Sam doesn't take the commitment lightly! The thing is that when Billy got to New London to go into sub school, the inducting officer turned out to be a guy who had vacationed in Charleston last year and spent a lot of time with Billy. Follow me so far?"

Berrigan nodded, intrigued by Corette's story.

"So Billy tells this officer-friend it's all a big mistake and now the officer is pulling some strings trying to get our boy Acorn off the hook. In the meantime, they're swinging up at the officers' quarters, laughing their heads off at the coincidence of meeting in New London!"

Corette finished her story with another burst of laughter that dislodged all the aches and miseries of Berrigan's travelogue.

Berrigan liked the easy company Corette offered, and urged her to talk about her art.

For many miles then, Corette discussed her first art courses, her failure to enjoy contemporary painters, her love of the tactile experience of sculpture.

"Clay is marvelous to squish in; plaster and wire are even better. There's something so satisfying in playing in a mess and creating form from it, into something recognizeable."

Corette also talked at length and with high praise for her mother's talent as a painter.

"She's well known in Vermont. Sort of their version of Georgia O'Keefe! When I was little, I never knew her to be without splashes of paint on her neck. Even at cocktail parties!"

Corette's most exciting news, even to share with a stranger, was her chance at getting an exhibition at a Virginia gallery.

"It's all speculation right now. But they're soliciting new young painters, so I sent a letter. My father went to school in that city; maybe some of his friends are still there."

Corette explained then that her father had died of heart disease four years ago.

"He was a Navy man, big on sailing."

Switching topics, Corette asked, "Is it safe to be hitching alone? Had any hassles with the people on the highway?"

"Not really."

"Maybe I should say the *men* on the highway."

"I've been lucky, I guess. No one has tried pulling off onto any side roads or anything like that. They all talk a fast game, but no one tried anything. But I've really been more preoccupied with my destination than with my traveling companions."

While they stopped for gas at a small town in New York state, four highway patrol cars and an ambulance with lights flashing were parked on the other side of the road. Crossing the highway to investigate, the two women saw a trooper just dropping a blanket over a young blonde girl, dressed in a blue and red school outfit. There was a large white "R" on her letter sweater. The troopers lifted her gently from where she had been found, her body twisted and lying askew in a ditch of tall grass by the highway.

"Anyone see anything?" one trooper asked.

"She's been tossed out of a semi," a boy answered.

"How do you know that, son?"

"I pump gas at the station over there. 'Bout half an hour ago, I saw a Danville Freight tandem-semi pull off here. He let his engines idle, oh, just a coupla minutes. Then he pulled out and drove off."

"Did you get a look at the driver?"

"Not a close one. He had black hair, I think, and glasses. That's all I could tell from across the highway. I was standing at the pump. I noticed him mainly because he didn't seem to have any

94

trouble. Just pulled off, and then on again. Most truckers stick to their schedules and don't waste any time. I'd lay 20-to-1 odds that trucker threw the girl out when he stopped, though."

"Looked like a cheerleader, don't you think, Will?" one trooper asked the other.

"She was probably late and thought she'd jump a ride to a game. Let's ask the station boy if there's a small school hereabouts. With an 'R' in the name."

"Damned truckers," the trooper started.

"Damned young girls with no sense," his partner said. "They don't expect danger. They trust everybody. Home-town friendliness, you know."

"*That* trucker was no home-town boy."

Berrigan and Corette watched the men move the girl towards the ambulance. Her foot protruded from underneath the blanket. There were no words that could save her now. As the troopers passed the two women, a blue sock bobbed lifeless behind them to the ambulance.

From the gas station to the Connecticut state line, the road burned in a static hum under the trusty Ambassador, but all conversation was lost in the vision of the blue sock. After passing one sign announcing the state line, Corette asked, "Are we getting close to where you want me to stop?" Berrigan didn't answer. Corette drove on several miles and then coasted off the road, putting her car into a shaky idle. Berrigan opened the car door immediately and stepped out, walking a few paces from the car as her tears streamed over her face. Time lost dimension momentarily as her thoughts filled with the image of the blonde girl's limp leg, her body like a wound in the green grass.

Corette broke into these thoughts: "Are you in a hurry to get home? It might take some help to get Billy Acorn out of the grips of the U.S. Navy. That is, if you're interested, if you want to go along with me."

Berrigan nodded, but couldn't turn to face Corette and answer directly.

"I'm going to check the water in this car before we go any further. If you hear a small explosion, don't panic. It always burps when I check the water."

Managing a weak laugh in response, Berrigan composed herself while the Ambassador squawked and burped.

On to New London!

The U.S. Navy nearly got Billy Acorn, as he explained breathlessly to Corette and Berrigan upon their arrival at the Naval Base Commander's Building.

"I hope you appreciate us, Billy Acorn!" Corette started out, waggling her finger at him while he tried to hug her. "Those damned sailors at the base gate wouldn't let us in until we promised to blow them around the block!"

"Oh, I hope you recommended me instead!"

"Of course! But seriously, Billy, are you in or out?"

"I came close, nearly *too* close for a proper nappie nellie, to losing my virginity to these crazy sailors! I swear, it was some scene! There I was, up in front of this officer, takin' my vows and the time came to say 'I do' and in walked my friend, Lt. Drawers, just in the nick of time! The sweat was on my neck, honey, and I don't mean *maybe*!

"Lt. Drawers started one helluva hullabaloo, goin' on about how this was some fool snafu caused by some asshole junior officer and that in fact, the man who was supposed to be inducted was named Ahorn instead of Acorn.

"Then he goes on to say, motioning to me, 'This man here has fatal phritis and is on his last legs anyway.' All the other guys started grabbing their crotches since none of 'em had ever heard of phritis and they thought it was some kind of sex disease! Oh man, it was hysterical!

"Then Drawers takes me out into the hall all super-cool and formal, and we burst out laughing! But it worked, babes! I am a free man again, delivered by the valiant Lt. Drawers from the grips of certain gang rape! And let me tell you, he's a sweet one, he is!"

"Don't believe this 'Mary Limp Wrist' act of Billy's, Berrigan. He's really a muscle-man in disguise."

"Whatever he is, he's unique! Would you two excuse me a minute? I've got to make a phone call."

"Okay, but look, this whole extravaganza calls for a celebration! Let's do up New London before we go. We've got to leave a marker for this historic event, an 'Acorn and Friends Were Here' bit."

"I'm calling a friend in Bingham. If she's free, can I ask her to join us?"

"Hell yes! The more the merrier!"

And so the unexpected duet that started on a dusty highway in Pittsburgh and became a disjointed trio in New London now expanded into a jumbled menagerie, as Evelyn drove in to join them, and Lt. Drawers finally appeared along with a six-foot-tall Amazonian escort. Drawers himself was the sailor on enlistment posters, except for full, over-red lips and minus the crew-cut.

Introducing his companion, he said, "This is Dewar, a WAVE-Lieutenant from New York. The women up there were driving her berserk in the barracks, so she came down here for an R & R."

"The boys always leave me alone," she responded, with a voice that would have made Garbo proud, and grinning with a wide mouthful of giant teeth.

Evelyn arrived about two hours after Berrigan's call, eager for the adventure and hugging Berrigan in warm reunion.

They all set out for the central New London tavern, The Gold

96

Bar Inn, for dancing, drinking, and stumbling until 2 A.M., through toasts to everything from freedom and the National Fleet to John Paul Jones and his "iron prick." Evelyn was friendly and interested in Dewar, who had been unanimated until they struck up conversation.

The party finally ended up in a rousing strip poker and boogie fest at Lt. Drawers' apartment. When everyone had lost everything and they were reduced to a staggering sextet of bodies wrapped in thrice-bid sheets, they retired to a reviving group-bath in Drawers' huge sunken tub.

In the haze of alcohol, none of them could have appreciated their Felliniesque parade of nudity to the tub:

*Dewar, with pelvic bones protruding like hip-wings below breasts hard and round as raw potato;

*Lt. Drawers, with his tight skinny butt and broad shoulders, marching into the water, his ample penis floating straight out from his body like a battleship;

*Evelyn, straight-faced and dramatic as she simulated a Valentino-tango step right into the water;

*Berrigan and Corette together, too tipsy to reach the water alone, giggling like cherubs, their soft buttocks bumping with small slap-slap sounds, their nut-brown nipples erect with the cold;

*And finally, "Shamrock Sally," in all his naked plumage: jive-walking, finger-snapping, doing the camel-walk bebop-a-lu-lah into the water, which made his black body shine in crystal spangles.

Eyes aching, head pounding, Berrigan emerged hours later. Over the edge of pain from her hangover, she awakened into the reality of the sturdy Ambassador back on the road, heading for Vermont. She vaguely remembered collecting her clothes and tumbling into the car with Billy, Corette, and Evelyn. Evelyn! She shook away the desire to slip back into groggy sleep and asked Billy, who was driving, *What have we done with Evelyn?*

He patted her and whispered, "Relax! She got a good night's sleep and then we drove her to her car. I'm sure she's safe and sound back in Bingham by now. You've been conked nearly twelve hours, kid!"

That was some party!

"That was some kind of powerful stuff they kept serving us at the Gold Bar Inn. 'Zap Juice' or something."

I hope you're satisfied. You definitely left your mark.

Billy began humming, and Berrigan began to let her senses ooze back into sleep.

Everyone surfaced at a diner many miles later. Hot food and enough sleep had worn off most of their post-party effects. Chuckling over some of their antics the night before, they marveled at Lt. Drawers' master scheme which had saved "Shamrock Sally" from a fate worse than death: "Two years in wool bell bottoms and Navy issue skivvys!"

"You'd have had to liquidate your feather boas and your lingerie collection," Corette chided Billy.

"Oh, it might not have been so bad, though. From what I hear of the rumors circulating about you, Mr. Acorn, in no time at all, you'd have had a 'boy in every port!' "

"Hopefully a descendant of John Paul Jones! But no matter. I got my share in New London anyway, which isn't bad for a week's visit."

"Is that what you'd call a 'lay-over'?" Corette asked, winking.

"Don't be so bitchy, Corette! It just means I haven't lost my touch. Ole 'Sally' is still the hottest rod in town!"

With that remark, Billy did a peppy dance right out of the booth, catching the attention of some of the other diners.

"I'll be sure and report your successes to our crew in Charleston, if that's what you're hoping for. Now sit down!"

"Tacky, tacky, Corette! You know I never brag!"

"Oh sure!"

"Lt. Drawers looked like quite a rod himself. At least, what I remember from the bath, even though I was really drunk."

"Even drunk, it would be hard not to notice *that* feature!" Corette put her hand on Berrigan's arm, sharing her laughter with her new friend.

"Big Boys are always fun to play with. But energy and style: that wins out over size everytime."

"What about gentleness?"

"Each to their own method, I guess!"

"Yes, yes, Billy, we all know you're a fine fast ram for the boys. But a 'sexual poet' you'll never be!"

They laughed and then the bill came and soon the Ambassador was pointing for "Corral Pablo," the studio owned by Corette's mother in Calais, Vermont.

* * * * * *

With Fortune her Mistress then, Berrigan was to have the great advantage of being able to learn and observe Corette and her mother at the same time. They were much alike, with Corette a younger version of her vibrant artist-mother, ValJean Hill. It was easy to trace Corette's exuberance for life and her liberal acceptance of humanity. All the personalities and idiosyncracies of humankind were allowed for and portrayed in ValJean's painting, with quick strokes in brilliant yellow swatches on grey suns. All the street faces Berrigan knew were there, as well as the smooth wealthy ones like herself and Corette, the restless and the frustrated, the desperate and doomed, children in discovery, lovers, parents, the decline of youth. All were given equal consideration in care of detail. Each spoke a message out of the canvas. Looking at them was like ingesting their dreams and aches as confidante. Berrigan wished that some day she could write characters as real as those in ValJean's art.

Both mother and daughter Hill had a way of taking people in, offering uninhibited affection and hospitality. They were not wary people, overly concerned with misconstrual. ValJean welcomed Berrigan in as another in Corette's troop, admitting she loved the variety of her daughter's friends.

"The people she attracts are inspiration for my art. Sometimes their expressions emerge from my brush unexpectedly."

The house-studio was spacious, open-beamed, with lots of room between the pieces of furniture. ValJean explained, "We're arranged here so that guests can stretch out and relax. If that means creativity for others as much as it does for me, then I'm encouraged."

The studio itself was garage-like, its concrete floor grown over with canvases on sawhorses and easels, some finished, some in process. From their position, it would seem ValJean often moved from picture to picture, as though all of them were connected at some point. She could capture a mood and mix a color and swipe across all of the paintings at once, taking in all of her creative projects. And yet, each was distinctly different in theme and design.

Berrigan noticed an abundance of books on Picasso strewn about, and partially covered over in one corner, attempts to copy several poses of his "Blue Nudes." When she asked ValJean if the studio, "Corral Pablo," was named after that master, her reply was effusive.

"Of course, of course! I wish I had his discipline and dedication! It was Corette who got me so interested in Picasso, by taking me to a special exhibit of his in Atlanta. They also showed a film of him at work, and I was hooked! When I get stale, I look into Picasso and always find a renewal of myself from his many themes. I have also learned to paint women better by studying his nudes. My copies are dreadful, but at the time I did them, they served to bring me out of a long period of stagnation, right after my husband died. I've been painting non-stop since then, so I keep them around to remind myself to stay alert and open. Sometimes my painting inspiration is fickle with me, secretive. It hides inside of me. How perplexing it is to have my glimpses of genius playing hide-and-seek within my own self!"

There was yet another artist in the Hill family, as Corette demonstrated to Berrigan several nights after their arrival at the studio. Walking into Corette's room, Berrigan found her new friend standing out on the terrace with her back to the door, staring into the dark Vermont sky. Night sounds and scents were filling the room, and Berrigan suddenly felt herself overcome with a need to know Corette, to be close to her. She started for the terrace but stopped, seeing an easel in the middle of the room. On it sat a canvas, its story recognizeable at once. Beseeching eyes stared out of the picture; the face ached with vulnerability. And in the background, a road ran up into the sky, kinetic with the whirring wheels of a tandem semi-truck. It was a painting of the high school girl they had seen at the roadside in New York. Corette had given her a face out of her imagination, an identity in a portrait of the essence of pain. Again Berrigan was beseiged with tears, both for the dead girl and for the sensitive way in which Corette had managed to strike the incident in paint. She left the room and the painting and Corette as soundlessly as she had entered.

The next morning when Corette got up and walked to the painting, to contemplate it again as she had done so many times during the night, she found a folded paper between one edge of the canvas and the easel. It was Berrigan's poem for the cheerleader.

For All the Lost Cheering

The American Queen at Seventeen: blonde and full of dreams.
She was late. Her friends had gone.
They would have the kickoff without her.
She ran up the road for a ride.

The truck was big and loud,
blowing like an angry whale.
"Danville Freight," it read on the side.
The license tag was blotted with dirt.

"Hi, Cutie Pie. Need a ride?"
(Want some candy, little girl? You're *real* sweet.)
"Need a ride?" she heard the driver say.
"Just to the fork; it's not far. I'm late for the game."
The door of the truck yawned wide open to her.
(Want some candy, little girl? You're *real* sweet.)

She pulled at the top of her blue sock,
watching the driver.
He was bouncing in the seat,
chewing his gum with a vengeance,
his eyes on her breasts
underneath the letter sweater.
She was spelling out the Victory cheer in her mind
As they drove and the truck groaned.

She missed the kickoff
and the first score
and the final touchdown
and all the cheering.
(Want some candy, little girl? You're *real* sweet.)

A hairy hand out of nowhere,
uninvited, unexpected,
strangled her face, pulled her hair,

100

invaded the letter sweater,
twisting and bending her like ragged twine.
She missed the Victory cheer.
She missed her stop at the fork.
"Danville Freight" with no visible tag
left her, in a ditch, her spirit bowed.
She smelled flying tar grit and her own blood.
She dreamed her last dream, spelling the Victory cheer.
"Need a ride?" she had heard him say.

At breakfast, Billy was eating alone. When Corette came downstairs from her room, she brought the canvas with her, though it was covered.

"Where's Mom?"

"She got an early start painting. Whatcha got there?"

"Nothing. Just an idea I started sketching last night."

"Let me see!"

"No, it's not finished yet. Don't be so impatient!"

Billy motioned upstairs with his eyes. "Your hitch-hiker up yet?"

"I'm not sure. Why don't you go walk the dogs?"

"Nice mood you're in this morning! You artists — all temperament and no tact!"

Billy left the room at Corette's urging just as Berrigan emerged.

"*Morning!*"

"Good morning. Want some hot cereal?"

Corette poured them both bowls of the cereal, and went about the business of diluting hers with brown sugar and milk. Berrigan noticed the canvas propped against the chair.

"*Did you show the painting to your mother?*"

"Not yet."

They ate in silence, both of them awkwardly obvious in not talking about the painting and the poem. Finally Berrigan said, "*You were up quite late, weren't you?*"

"You weren't asleep yourself, I guess."

They stopped eating at the same time, and grinned.

"I don't even like hot cereal."

"*I liked your painting very much.*"

"Your poem moved me. It was a special gift."

They were awkward again for a moment, diverting their eyes from each other.

"*You know, I don't like hot cereal either.*"

Alone at the table, they grinned again, sharing the secret of their creativity. Corette reached across the table to Berrigan, and they clasped hands.

* * * * * *

The time at the studio was a holiday for Berrigan. She felt her optimism bolstered in the warm, affectionate atmosphere. They all took walks with ValJean's Corgis, Ned and Chip, in a meadow near the studio. Berrigan especially enjoyed ValJean's company.

"ValJean, I'm having such a wonderful time. I can't tell you how much it's meant to me to be here."

"I'm glad you feel that way. I guess my theory about 'stretching room' does work. Corette tells me you're a poet. Sometime I'd like to see what you've written."

"Perhaps you should rename the studio 'Place of good cheer.'"

"I appreciate your kindness, Berrigan."

"I can see where Corette gets her artistic bent."

"Corette doesn't paint often, but when she does, I'm always amazed by the emotion released within her pictures. You're sensitive like her, and that makes you her old friend right away. You're both easy women to be around."

"How long has Billy been part of the family?"

"He came home with Corette about three years ago. She was in drama school in Charleston and he was in the troupe there. He's only a 'jive bunny' on the surface. Corette had a knack for recognizing that. I think now he comes here to get re-charged."

"Yes, and maybe to rest!"

ValJean laughed with that same kind of lightness Berrigan reacted to in Corette on the Pittsburgh highway.

"One day he'll find himself. In the meantime, I welcome him."

They smiled, looking into one another's faces. Then ValJean called the Corgis in to walk back to the studio, her arm looped through Berrigan's.

The week in Calais ended, and once again, Billy, Corette, and Berrigan were facing the familiar hum of the road in the eccentric Ambassador. As they were saying goodbyes with ValJean, she asked Corette, "Do you think you'll get back okay in this old car?"

"Sure, Mom," Corette said, patting the car. "It's a faithful beast, like a tired lion: it's old and shaky, but it still gets through the jungle!"

On that note, the three drove away from the studio, leaving ValJean standing under the arch and the "Corral Pablo" sign. Ned and Chip were barking and jumping at her while she waved until the car crested a hill, out of sight.

"Are the dogs your mother's only companions?" Berrigan asked.

"Oh, no! There's a retired sea captain who lives on the next acreage. He serves as Mother's 'platonic escort.' "

"The noble, self-effacing Captain Jack," Billy offered cryptically from the backseat.

"Okay, Billy, now don't start in on that theory of yours that Jack is a closet fag whose social reputation is fulfilled by my mother. Spare me that starting this long trip back."

Berrigan felt a slight tension in Corette's tone which briefly silenced further comments from Billy.

"Mother and Jack are happy with their arrangement and that's the most important thing. Her art is her life; it has been ever since my father died. She's fulfilled and happy as an artist."

"Has she thought of marrying again?"

"She says her marriage with my father was one of a kind, and her life would be frustrated searching for another like it. She told me that my father always encouraged her to be her own person. Now her painting is her focal point, and she sells well in Vermont. It's a disciplined life, but one that she's adjusted to."

"Yes, yes, but don't you worry about her sexual psyche?" Billy persisted.

"My god, Billy, she's 54 years old! She can take care of her own psyche, with no help from you!"

Billy's scathing wit wilted. The game was over; he'd struck at a tender spot in Corette's family and she answered him on sharp terms. Corette allowed Billy a flippant dependency on her, but there were times when he apparently ignored his limits.

The rest of the trip to Connecticut went rapidly. Billy and Corette ignored the terse conversation they'd had and joked with each other amiably, arguing without anger over whether to listen to soul music or classical on the radio. They compromised, singing their own rendition of "The Blue Danube" as Billy beat the car seat like a tom-tom and interjected a "baby oh baby" background to Corette's melody. Berrigan added a third part to their disharmony with "do wacka doo" every sixth beat. They all decided Strauss would definitely be turning over in his grave.

"I could use this in my routine!" Billy exclaimed. "You know, Corettte, in my number with the feather boas!"

Before she was ready, Berrigan was in Bingham at Evelyn's house, bidding her new companions farewell.

"I want you to come to Charleston!" Corette told her, "I'll write you!"

"For sure! Take care, now. And especially look out for this one!" Berrigan pointed to Billy, who grinned out from under his red afro.

The Ambassador chugged and coughed down Bingham's main street back towards the highway, with Corette's call fading, "See ya later, alligator!"

Berrigan watched until there was only the quiet street and the conversation of neighborhood dogs for company.

(Home again, home again, ho hum a holiday!)

Suddenly, Berrigan thought that she didn't even get Corette's address in Charleston. What if Corette didn't write? It was very important to know she would be back in touch with Corette. Berrigan felt a crazy urge to run down the street and overtake their car. She pictured herself banging on the car, *"Let me in, let me back in, Corette!"* The sting of tears brought her back to her senses.

103

(What's the matter with me? For Paulasakes!)

Berrigan picked up her bag and pack and went into the house, anticipating Evelyn's surprise at finding the second army cot occupied once again.

* * * * * *

The apartment was undoubtedly Evelyn's: clothes were strewn everywhere, the bedding was half on the floor, and the kitchen was a disaster area.

(My God, Evelyn Walker, you do need a keeper!)

Berrigan began to gather some of the clothes together, sorting through the mayhem. Lifting up one of Evelyn's blouses, she uncovered a letter lying open. As she placed it on Evelyn's desk, she saw that it had Daniel Norman's signature on it. But Berrigan didn't give herself time to be tempted, leaving the letter gingerly on the desk. Working at her restoration project, 182 sighs and 45 minutes later, a path was cleared and Berrigan flopped onto one of the army cots.

(Eveyln, you'll never graduate past discount beer or to real mattresses. What am I going to do with you?!)

Despite constant questions and prodding from Berrigan, Evelyn had not revealed anything further on the promising affair she wrote about to Berrigan in St. Louis. She had moved into her own apartment, but from the looks of things, all the chaos belonged to Evelyn alone. Berrigan was sure Evelyn was seeing someone but she didn't understand her friend's reticence about discussing her love life. There had never been secrets between them when they lived together and Berrigan's correspondence was always vivid with the events of her own life. Perhaps a greater privacy of self was a direction Evelyn was moving into. But for whose protection?

As she rested in Evelyn's apartment, Berrigan reviewed those few brief comments from Evelyn's letters. She began to worry and wondered what Evelyn could be up to. Was there trouble with her parents? Was the new paramour a drinker? A violent personality? Poor? A woman? A Jew? All manner of fantastic possibilities swirled through Berrigan's thoughts.

Then she remembered the letter she had seen while cleaning the apartment. She went to the desk and picked it up to read, without analysis of her motives or rationalization for her invasion of Evelyn's privacy.

> "Dear Ev: I miss you, dear. Am only waiting for an invitation to return. In the meantime, I am burning a midnight taper and playing mournful songs. Please let me hear from you soon.
>
> > Remember me,
> > Daniel Norman."

The letter was postmarked from Hartford. Berrigan's heart

gave a lurch at the plea she read in this short message as she wondered about Daniel and Evelyn.

Before she could muse any further without Evelyn in person, she appeared, momentarily speechless when she saw the clean apartment and more so as there was Berrigan, smiling at her with Daniel's letter in her hand.

Berrigan put the letter down on the desk and went to Evelyn.

"Well say hello, stranger!"

Evelyn laughed and hugged Berrigan, spinning her around until they both nearly collapsed into the army cots.

"Careful!"

"What the hell are you doing here without letting me know so I could have at least put a clean sheet on your cot?"

"There really wasn't time to let you know when I'd be here after I left Vermont. Besides, I wanted to surprise you! But now I don't know if it was me or my staving off the approaching menace of chaos in this apartment that got to you most!"

"It was you, Berrigan, of course. It's always been you."

Evelyn walked to the desk and put her books down, glancing at the letter to see what Berrigan had been reading.

"So! Let's get some supper on, okay? I didn't have the energy to do anything about the kitchen so I don't really know what you've got in there. Anything we can salvage? Or has it all turned to gunpowder?"

"Did you find this reading material interesting?"

Evelyn's question was not sarcastic or defensive, but a genuine and direct query. Berrigan didn't answer, but stopped at the kitchen door, not turning back to Evelyn.

"Daniel's letter, I mean," she persisted.

Berrigan turned back to her. *"Yes. I discovered it accidentally, uncovering it while I was cleaning. I know I had no right to read it."*

"I'm actually glad you found the letter. There's so much I want to share with you but I wasn't sure where or how to begin. This breaks the ice for me."

"Have I become so hard to talk to?"

Evelyn laughed and went to Berrigan and hugged her again. Planting a noisy kiss on her lips, she then slouched down on one of the cots.

"God no, Berrigan. You're about the only person I *can* talk to! It's just that my mind and emotions have been in such turmoil. My grasp on things hasn't been coherent and the opportunity to tell you my feelings in person just hasn't been right. I didn't want it all to come out sounding like confused goulash!"

"I don't have to ask if you've got beer. Let's have some and you can tell all!"

Evelyn grinned sheepishly and they headed for the kitchen, arm-in-arm, holding each other warmly. Later, as they lay side by side in the army cots sharing a cigarette and a six-pack, Evelyn was able to open up about her relationship with Daniel Norman.

"I met Daniel here at the college; he's a music major. Something about him was different, comfortable. He wasn't a jock or some brainy pre-med jerk or like any other guy I've seen. He was not intimidated by my family name or the money or Daddy.

"We started studying together and then just being together and before I knew it, we were living here together. I guess what freaked me out was that it felt so right I just didn't stop to question what we were doing.

"For the first time, a man loved me for *me*. And I'm not the easiest person to live with. I'm messy, AC-DC about my father's money, ambitious about a career. I'm not one of those instantly lovable passive wife candidates. I haven't worn a spaghetti-strapped gown out to dinner in years!"

"Face it, Ev. You're losing touch with the upper class!"

"Daniel and I split about three weeks ago. He went to Hartford to try to get into the symphony orchestra. He's a brilliant flautist and I know he'll get the position. But I needed the time to sort things out."

" How has your family responded?"

"They were less than jubilant, as you can imagine. Walker women do not live with men out of wedlock. Especially a man who is neither doctor, lawyer, or Indian chief. Daniel is never going to be rich or a young executive or a leader of men. My father has his doubts about the manliness of a flute player. Obviously they don't understand my interest."

"Do you understand it?"

"It's so simple it's taken me six months to figure it out. Daniel is not the kind of man I thought I'd take to my bed, much less to my heart. He's sensitive, quiet, self-contained. He doesn't want anything from me except my love."

"So what is he, a saint?"

"No, I don't mean that. I guess what I'm trying to say is that loving him doesn't interfere with me being me. I don't have to put on that spaghetti-strapped gown to get his attention or to please him. He encourages me to do more than cook a great pot roast."

"He's also nothing like Daddy, right?"

"He's no push-over though, Berrigan. He's not a weakling. But he's not a prick either. He's willing to admit it when he starts acting like a little boy needing Mama, or a chauvinist."

"From his letter, he finds Hartford lonely. He wants to get back together with you."

"I like having him here. And I want to be with him. I'm going to ask him to come back. I don't know where it goes from there."

"If you thought I'd be jealous, you're right! I don't like the idea of someone else sleeping in my cot or reaping the direct benefits of your special self. But right now, I'm more hungry than jealous.

106

Evelyn, I love you. And I'm willing to welcome any partner in your life. But now, feed me, please!"

And so the willing camaraderie, sewed over countless sips of sudsy and sights into the same pains, restored them to one another, reinforcing their special private line of communication.

Berrigan's Journal – August 28

Evelyn and I have spent several days briefing each other about the last few months. She's helped me relax about being home again.

I went to see Mom and Dad today. They're okay. They were disconcerted that I have written so little and that I am staying with Evelyn. But none of this was stated directly to me. I read it in their slouching inflections, in tones loose at the ends and trembly. Mother has gained six pounds and won't stop fussing over it. Dad is wrestling distractedly with the electrical problem of keeping all the fuses in the house from blowing when he runs his power saw at the same time as Mother runs the TV.

They asked how things were in St. Louis, and it was hard to discuss that without revealing the whole situation with Mac and the bars. They wanted to know what kind of work I did, and of course, if I had any money.

"Did you date any of those fancy St. Louis men?" Dad asked, winking. Mother wanted to know if I had heard that Syru Cox made the Bingham Spoiler headlines by leading a picket line at the State House. Evelyn hadn't mentioned it in any of her letters, although she did say Syru had resurfaced in Bingham. As for the picket, it seems Syru discovered that legislative secretaries are paid less than State House janitors and so she got the secretaries organized and up in arms, protesting. With this news of her renewed activism, I realize how muffled my consciousness of events outside my own personal realm has been in the last months.

When I left Mom and Dad, I wanted to hold on to them a little when we hugged, because I do love them. But I come between us, what I am, essentially. Loving women makes me happy; it would be a source of unending trauma for them to try to comprehend. So at best, I wish to be pleasant, but this is at the expense of being personal and honest. I lose my family to gain myself, and it makes me sad. Back here at the apartment, I cried, because I can't seem to change things for us. That is probably selling me short; I ought to have the faith Syru does, in the resource of women and in myself.

But I know something isn't at rest in me, not just with the folks, but with Evelyn too, with my whole attitude. It's like having a dream so vivid I want to remember it and just can't, so I keep searching my own mind, straining to recall the dimensions of the dream. That's my sensation, and it's an urgent one. But what is the dream?

Berrigan's Journal — August 29
Got up early this morning and walked to Amil's. He was surprised to see me and gave me a hug and a slap on the back, nearly whacking the breath out of me. He's the same old stubbornly lovable character; he told me all the neighborhood gossip, pulling me up against his white apron with one huge arm around me.

We had a bagel and a large warty pickle and he told me all the improvements he's made on the store. As I was leaving, he pointed to his new checker, a sincere-looking high school girl.

"See? I'm doing all right, aren't I?"

I winked and squeezed his fat fingers.

Berrigan's Journal — August 30
Evelyn and I have decided to go up to Uncle David's farm. He and his family are on vacation and since it's Saturday, I know their hired man will be in Bingham at the tavern. We'll have the place to ourselves then; I can always ruminate better in the country. I often feel cloistered from myself by city pressures, even one the size of Bingham. Maybe all these bodies run interference with my own energies? Then too, the farm is full of memories for me. Maybe my recent elusive "dream" will finally unveil for me out there.

Corette called just as we were leaving! The connection was bad and the line crackled constantly and I had to ask her to repeat everything she said. It was so good to hear her voice!

She told me that on her return to Charleston, the Ambassador stalled twice and Billy suggested driving it to the beach and into the water for burial at sea.

"I guess I should get rid of that car, but it has such character, such loyalty. That's got to count for something!"

She's excited because the gallery in Virginia wants her to submit some work to them. They've chosen her as a finalist for a showing. She says she's painting up a storm.

As we were signing off, I got Corette's address, and she ended our talk with her signature slogan: "See ya later, alligator!"

Corette's lack of preoccupation with small miseries, her ability to ignore irritations, her sureness of direction — makes me feel a little ridiculous with myself. After her call, I relaxed about my own dismay, able to look forward to a good time with Evelyn at the farm.

*   *   *   *   *   *

In their jeans and work shirts, Evelyn and Berrigan walked the perimeter of the farm, crossing the fields and catching stickers in their cuffs. Evelyn carried a six-pack of her favorite bargain beer. They examined the ruins of a rusty combine, and climbed a steep embankment to survey the acreage. Berrigan explained to

Evelyn how her uncle usually planted, where he kept his livestock, sharing some of her memories she had of her visits. They were happy for the chance to be together at play away from Bingham.

They tried to fly a kite in a meadow just across the road from the farmhouse. Evelyn managed to get the kite skyborn, but when Berrigan took the string, the wind left them and the fragile craft of sticks and paper went into a rapid nose-dive, breaking upon impact. Berrigan shrugged at Evelyn's teasing scolds and yelled good-naturedly when she was showered with beer from a can Evelyn had shaken.

They talked to each other like Ma n' Pa Kettle, Evelyn being the better pretender: she kept spitting as though she had a mouth full of tobacco. "See that'n, Ma?" she said, snickering. "Musta been two feet!"

Finally they walked with their arms around each other's waists down to the stream, where they rolled up their pantslegs to wade. After a rock skimming contest, they began wrestling on the creek bank and both lost their balance, falling into the water.

With the house locked, they went up into the loft to strip down and towel off. Evelyn was drying Berrigan's hair. Berrigan noticed the gentleness in her friend's touch. She diverted her attention to the loft.

"Uncle David used to keep a mule in here, and pigs. Their gossip would make a great story for you to write, Evelyn. I've been in this loft before."

Evelyn's thoughts were not on this suggested expose, as she commented, "I've never noticed before, Berrigan, but you have great shoulders."

She walked to the window and stood there, looking out, her nudity silhouetted by the bright sun. Berrigan looked at the towel draped in the crook of Evelyn's arm, and at the golden frame of sun around her body.

They were naked together in a way different from being just good friends or roommates and both of them knew it; the two women seemed to have the same thought for a moment and did not ignore it but rather tripped over each other remarking. "You know what I was just thinking . . .?"

"You lesbians are all alike!"

"Works both ways, honey!"

They laughed and sat down in the loft window, dangling their legs out over the barnyard, watching the chickens scratching for grain, their heads bobbing, their feet lifted and placed down again precisely.

"Who would believe it?" Berrigan said, breaking their hypnotic observation of the feeding chickens.

"What?"

"The Bingham Spoiler Scandal Sheet would never believe we were up in a deserted loft naked and neither of us suggesting a roll in the hay!"

"Are you disappointed?"

"The only thing that disappoints me is the general misconception that deep friendship is empty without sex. What bullshit!"

"We are what we have always been, Berrigan. I'm glad we know our focus, even though the world does not. I'm not afraid to say I love you, but I don't want to sleep with you."

"And I'm not afraid to say I love you, but I don't need to sleep with you."

They considered, silently and separately, a fearful and confused world and the narrow attitudes about women loving each other.

"Just never say 'never'!" Berrigan said, grinning.

"Okay. How about 'maybe someday'?" Evelyn responded.

"Here's to my favorite aqua deb!"

"Here's to my favorite Wonder Woman!"

Laughing and hugging, they dressed, ate their picnic lunch, and consumed the remainder of Evelyn's beer. Evelyn was full of questions about the farm animals, telling Berrigan she had always secretly wished to be Rebecca of Sunnybrook Farm.

"I wanted to go gather the eggs, you know."

"Oh sure! I can imagine! Rustic fantasies from Ft. Knox!"

Around 3:00, Evelyn packed up the picnic basket and headed for the car alone, leaving Berrigan in the loft for one last reminiscence of the farm. Berrigan leaned back in the loft window, banging her feet in dull thumps against the barn. The chickens scattered at the sound. The sun beat down on the field. Berrigan looked into the glare and suddenly saw Corette's face. The image startled her and she closed her eyes. Opening them again, she saw only the sun and the chickens regrouping. She knew it was time to go.

On the way to the car, she stopped inside the barn, listening to the wind in the hay, the flap of a peeling shingle. There were piles of dried manure in Bernard the mule's stall, and humps of earth where the sows had laid, having their piglets on cold starless nights. The antsy untouchable feeling of the pressing question, the dream to dissect, came back upon Berrigan. She felt no answer and turned to go, hearing the wind try to fool her with a sound like Beverly's giggle from the loft.

* * * * * *

Berrigan's Journal - September 1

Evelyn has gone to work, grumbling about the sunburned nose she got at the farm yesterday. I'm at her kitchen table, with time to put down some thoughts before I leave this to check out all the travails of trivia in the plot of my favorite soap-opera.

In front of me, in between our breakfast plates, is a yellowing folder of pictures that I found in a trunk in the barn. I must have left it there on one of my many visits as a child. In it are pictures of schoolmates, their teeth missing, their hairstyles chopped and

110

greased. All the pictures are signed on the back, in large **unintel**-ligible scrawls. I remember some of the faces and laugh at deciphering part of a long-forgotten corny gradeschool passion on the back of one of the large photos.

There are pictures of me here too, with my arm around a best friend, or in poses grinning, leaping, dashing, caught mid-air jumping a fence, letting a dog lick my face, and one with my hand in a cookie-jar. "The theif red-handed," I penciled on the back, "1959."

I remember how much I loved to work with Uncle David in the cow barn, where the smell of dung and milk was strong and the cows were warm. Some licked me with their huge pink scratchy tongues and one bit a chunk out of my buttock that left a permanent dent.

And now this morning, I am also looking at another folder of pictures, these more recent, from an album I left at my parents'. Again I pose with my arm around Nonnie, my best friend in high school. And there are other shots: a picture of Rusty Michaels, the black all-state wrestling champion who stole my heart with his wide open smile and his courtesy. My parents suffered grievously over the news that we were seen together having sodas. There's a picture of me in my prom dress, letting Rouster, one of the many family dogs, lick me; and here I am at my cousin Carole's wedding. Steve Keller came through the reception line six times just to see if I'd let him french kiss me without making a scene.

There are also several snaps of Linda Framer and me, squirting each other with a water hose while washing Evelyn's car; showing our "gams" together in my parent's porch swing; wearing BC sweatshirts — hers saying "Captain," and mine saying "Mate."

How different these eras and pictures. The dogs have all gone to dog heaven, my family is beyond me, and there are no friends, only lost lovers. Except for Evelyn. And Corette? She comes to my mind; how clear was the image of her in the sun on the field at the farm. Was she sending me a dream?

I wonder why I have no pictures of Syru. There seemed no time when she was still long enough to capture her, even in a quick photo. But I have pictures of her in my mind that are enough, some more striking in their poses and more brilliant in their colors than any camera could afford.

The stove timer just went off — time to see how the world turns!

Berrigan's Journal - September 5

Went clothes shopping with my Mother today; she is as constant as the sands of time, offering me dresses with Peter Pan collars, or blouses with small delicate buttons. I go to the racks and find more practical items, those that bear active wearing: double-layered knits, wide-bell beige slacks, a blue shirt with button-down collar, a red pullover vest.

"This is 'good looking casual,' Mother. Unflairful, but long lasting," I tell her and she smiles dimly, going to a rack in her own size, judging me difficult.

Then on a sale rack I spotted a lavender-print blouse, just like the one Corette was wearing when she let me in her car on the Pittsburgh highway. I touched it, held the sleeve, thinking of her painting and my poem.

Holding the sleeve of a sale-rack blouse, near my mother who was humming and sliding hangers one by one down the clothes rack, I realized I am in love with Corette Hill. I came home, sat on my army cot, and wrote her a long letter, telling her about my visit to the farm, about Evelyn, about Syru, about St. Louis, about me and my family and my dismay. Then I sealed it in an envelope, addressed it, and put it on Evelyn's desk with no intention of mailing it. It was a good release to write out all my feelings but I'm sure Corette has enough to deal with without including my life story!

Berrigan's Journal - September 10

Letter from Corette today. I ripped into it as if I thought the answer to Doomsday was contained inside, surprised by my own enthusiasm. She writes so that I can feel her lighthearted gayness, enjoy her jokes about Billy and a description of singing "Dixie" with a drunken lady in flea-market trappings, the two of them sitting on a curb on Rainbow Street.

"You can imagine what historians and City Fathers might have thought if they'd found us there! But we'd have been a great tourist attraction!"

When I finished reading, I went to the desk to get the letter I wrote last week, and it was gone.

I asked Evelyn tonight if she'd seen my letter; she mailed it.

Berrigan's Journal - September 17

Sitting around the apartment, bored with TV, can't write, have been doodling; phone rang three times with wrong numbers, but I kept thinking it might be Corette calling again.

I finally took a walk on the deserted Bingham College campus, about 6:30. I could hear a saw running in the ag. building, cars honking on the bridge over to the dorms. The buildings seem less imposing in the twilight; they sag in quiet sighs and blink drowsy windows at me.

Walking through the trees, in this hour when the sun moves towards the stars and leads us towards gradual darkness, I was pursued by an illusion, a hallucination, a ghost playing jokes on me. I felt this presence following me. Whenever I turned to look behind me, I thought I saw the lavender blouse and Corette's image eluding me, stepping behind trees, around the corners of buildings, out of view of windows.

112

Home again later I wrote this poem. I think what I saw was my own desire to escape facing my feelings about Corette, because I am so unsure if there is any chance of sharing them with her.

> Nymph of spirit
> in me burning
> night-desires across my day,
> Nymph of spirit
> in me turning
> narrow rips along my way:
> Free this space in me burning,
> Free desires in me turning,
> Yield an answer for my yearning!
> Let Corette unbind my fetters,
> Find me writing her love letters.

* * * * * *

Berrigan's Journal — September 20

Corette called. "You must come to Charleston! Billy's gone to Atlanta and I'm so lonely. I'm painting a blue-streak but I need company. Will you come?"

In a daze, I fumbled with packing, as Evelyn helped me, grinning, shouting, and urging, "Go, go!"

And so I am, three hours later, on a bus, my bags packed, my heart pumping with fear and expectation, heading for Charleston and Corette.

Is that the tires or my head humming, *"Hello, Hello, Hello?"*

Chapter 7

Some hours later, the bus slammed to a stop to avoid hitting a palsied black woman crossing the street. The jolt awakened Berrigan, who had finally succumbed to exhaustion. The sleep left her with an aching shoulder and a stiff neck. Stretching, she focused on the early fall Charleston morning, bright and crisp. As the bus traveled past the famous "Rainbow Street" where Corette had sung her rendition of "Dixie," Berrigan looked over the sea wall, watching two catamarans bob in the water and the criss-cross of a minesweeper out on drill. One of the sailors on the bow waved and the bus driver honked back at him. Any minute they would be at the station and once again Berrigan would be with Corette. There was really no other place she wished to be.

At the station dock, Berrigan dragged her bulging suitcase from the bus, as she searched the faces for Corette. Way down at the other end of the terminal, she spotted the lavender shirt and Corette running towards her, waving and shouting.

"I can't wait to show you Charleston," Corette told her later as they drove the Ambassador to her apartment. "There are a million fun things to do here."

"Is this place really so different from anywhere else? Is it better than Vermont?"

"It's like any other metro area, Berrigan. You can see some of the same empty faces and ragged lives as in Detroit or Miami or Atlanta. Every city has its skeletons, Berrigan; you know that. So standing over the grave staring at them won't make any difference. The bones won't gather together and disappear. So perk up! You're here to have a good time, as my escort in adventure!"

"Sorry, but I don't have a red afro."

"It wouldn't fit you anyway. I'm really glad you're here. Don't spoil it by being defensive. Just be yourself."

"I'm sorry, Corette, but I've been to Bingham in the meantime."

"Is home such a bad place?"

"Oh, I guess I get to the point where I think it is. I've missed the 'free fall' feeling I got used to with you and Billy in Vermont."

"Now that's more like it! Relax and let yourself free fall again. I think you'll be sold on Charleston!"

Berrigan's Journal — September 22

How could I be so terrible? I don't know what came over me at the station. But when Corette reached me, breathless, with her eyes shiny and her hair smelling like hawaiian ginger, I had such a rush of jealousy! My visit seemed to be to take Billy's place, and god knows, he doesn't deserve Corette. I guess I felt used, not here for who I am but as *his* substitute.

Of course that's ridiculous. I see that now. Corette could not be more attentive or accommodating. She's given up her bed for me, bunking on the couch in the main room down below. Her bedroom sits on a raised platform reached by a ladder, some decorator's idea of the "loft look."

Her apartment has that Hill trademark: "stretching room." Besides a large spool table and couch in the living room, and this bedroom, there is little else to clutter up Corette's thoughts except for a few bookcases. She's built a bench into one wall where she dabbles with silverwork; in the back of the kitchen is a desk where she writes and keeps personal papers, and out on her enclosed patio sit easels and paints as well as a potter's wheel. Besides the patio off the kitchen, there is also a huge sundeck facing the living room. Corette has stored there about eight canvases she is planning to send to the Virginia gallery.

"I never lack for creative space," Corette said when we got here and I walked through the house. She also told me that when she first moved in, everything was so full of dust that she choked for days.

"Whenever I sat down, the cushions gave off little coughs of dust that nearly did me in!"

The apartment sits over the studio of an artist-friend of Val-Jean's who is taking a working vacation in Paris. Corette pays no rent because she keeps up the maintenance.

As soon as I sat my bag down, Corette began telling me about her life in Charleston. She continued this monologue throughout the day, even eating apple slices and scrambled eggs (which she called "art muck") on the edge of the tub as I soaked out my aches and the travel grime. She continued nonstop as I dressed and then while I took my turn at food. We ended up driving down to the beach, where we walked among scores of muscley blond beach-bum types and executives out for a quick tan, their poochy midriffs red and puffy from overexposure.

There we met Dee Crane. She was bringing in her boat and had asked Corette to meet her and help load it on the trailer. Not a boat fan (my own lack of experience), I was still impressed with Dee's catamaran. She rode it right on to the sand, nearly dumping herself in the process. Jumping off the canvas deck, she offered a tan hand and a quick smile.

We managed to load the boat onto the trailer, although in removing the unwieldy aluminum mast, it wavered above Corette and slid too fast through her hands. The rest of the day she nursed skinned palms.

"Do you sail?" Corette asked me later. When I told her no, she offered, "Want to learn?"

115

"Sure!"

I've been reading about "flying" catamarans and I'd love to try it, even at the expense of a rough dunking. Like Evelyn, Corette makes me feel that I can do anything I want to if I am only willing to learn.

* * * * * *

Corette's pattern of living was established for Berrigan that first day in Charleston; activities sprouted on the spur of the moment when the impulse struck. Their pace, while leisurely, was interlaced with dashes here and there: to see people, sunsets, special films, high tide, the season's final catamaran regatta. Corette took Berrigan out on Dee's boat several times, teaching her sailing basics, and the all-important principle of balance on the canvas deck. Corette spoke about her father each time they went out; he was responsible for most of her knowledge of sailing.

"Watch the hulls carefully, Berrigan. If one dips under, we're sunk!"

On their third outing, they finally managed to fly a hull. They streaked across the water laughing and whooping like old salts, oblivious to the drenching spray.

One afternoon the two women spent in downtown Charleston, adventuring: chanting with a group of hare krishna men, their shaven heads bobbing to the beat of their drum, their loose togas rippling as they moved to the song. Farther on down the street, Berrigan and Corette stopped to rap with three tall black men selling silver bracelets and rings to raise money for the Afro-American League. Besieged by sidewalk preachers squawking promises of salvation through scratchy microphones, they peddled revivalist leaflets to innocent passersby. "Blessed be, blessed be," they droaned, pushing the leaflets into hands, pockets, and shopping sacks, then collapsing into laughter with gay irreverence.

These outings were always accompanied by talk, endless dialogues between Corette and Berrigan: opinions, observation, personal experience, theory, predictions, the formation of new possible philosophies. One topic they spent many hours considering was Civil War history. Berrigan was dismayed, visiting the buried forts in and around Charleston, notably Fort Sumter.

"I can't imagine the era of the Civil War, when all this beautiful country was torn up and pitted with cannonball craters."

"I know," Corette agreed. "No matter how much I read about how it all happened, the politics and power-plays, every time I look at these magnificent pillared houses, I have to remember there's a slave pit under the kitchen. I toured a plantation once when I first moved here, and when we looked down into the pit, voices of the ghosts poured out of the clay walls, filling me up with the grief of Southern history. Of course, that's probably a very naive Northern perception."

116

"*Do you think you could have fought for either side?*"

"It's hard for me to envision myself killing another person for any reason. However, fighting for freedom of choice is something I understand, intellectually."

"*Especially since as women we have to fight for that right every day.*"

"Emotionally though, killing for any reason is entirely foreign to me. I think it would be impossible for me."

"*No exception?*"

Corette paused a moment. "Maybe *one* . . . rape."

In unison, their minds clicked onto the memory of the blue sock, the wound in the green grass, the tragedy of the dead cheerleader.

Berrigan's Journal — October 7

Corette and I sat up tonight toasting marshmallows over a stove burner, lamenting that it will have to be spring before we can sail again. She speaks as though I will be here, as though I am here for good. Later, on the couch, with our bare feet curled up under us, Corette said, "Tell me about Berrigan."

So I spent the next four-and-a-half hours telling her about Nonnie, Linda, Syru, Mac, my parents, Evelyn, Doris, my years with boys like Dick Tyrell (their motives and their minds obnoxiously one dimensional). She got the whole schlemiel! I concluded, *"I've really picked the winners, haven't I? Doris would be disappointed."*

Corette gathered her thoughts and reactions to what I'd told her before she responded.

"When I got your letter telling me much of this, I wished I were close enough to shake you. Mourning the past and your mistakes is selfish and narcissistic; it wastes the present. You've learned by giving your strength to others, letting them lean on you. You've managed to keep just enough strength for yourself, but you don't realize it. You still need to get the confidence to do one thing, the kindest action of all: pick the ultimate winner . . . *you*. Someday I'm going to ask you again, 'Tell me about Berrigan.' Let it be a happy story with only happy endings. And you must make the endings come true. It's time — you owe yourself."

Berrigan's Journal — October 19

We went out sailing again today; Corette talked about her father and what a closed person he had seemed to be with her, except when they were sailing.

"It was as if the sea was his confidant and he wasn't afraid to open up when we were on the water."

Berrigan's Journal — October 24

Corette and I had a discussion tonight about female artistry trying to survive in a misogynist culture. She is so adept at expressing herself. Her objectivity stretches the boundaries of my thinking; I get revelations coming lickety split through my brain. She elates me!

I want to . . . to make a film together, write a book, put out a newspaper, spread the news, start a renaissance with the women who are our repressed and forgotten artists! Corette makes me feel that we can conquer all the distrust!

* * * * * *

A month is a long visit with anyone, but Corette seemed not to notice how the weeks had slipped away. The last week in October, she got a card from Billy. He would be home in four days. Reading the card aloud to Berrigan, they both laughed at his jokes and style: "My god, he's even a jive writer!"

But the note drew attention to the necessity for decision. Would Berrigan stay? Would she go back to Bingham to look for work? Complications were immediate: Berrigan didn't want to return to Bingham unless she could live with Evelyn, and Daniel was now back with her. Berrigan had not been invited to live with Corette and she had no idea what work she could find in Charleston. It had been nearly four months since she had worked, and her finances were staring an overdraft in the face.

"Screwoggs," Corette said, using her favorite expletive. "I suppose this means you'll leave?"

"I need to get a job somewhere."

"But you can't go! We've got a sailing date in the spring! Stay here in Charleston with me. We'll find work together. I need to get my own bank account in the black."

"I've already overstayed my welcome. Besides, you'll need the space for Billy."

"He doesn't *live* here! He only spends the night occasionally when he's too drunk to get back to his own apartment, or when he's depressed."

"Yeah, but he depends on your being available. I don't want to cramp your style."

"Maybe that's what Billy needs. He's too used to coming here whenever he wants to."

"But you're the one who needs to change that, not me or my being here. I don't want to be anyone's competition."

"I didn't mean that. I guess what I really mean is that Billy's here so much because I haven't found other company in Charleston that I prefer more than his. Your being here has been the best time I've known since I moved here. Now *you're* my preferred company! I just didn't know I was going to have to import you from Bingham!"

"I want to stay, but I'm not sure I want to take the risk. Living together is sometimes a quick way to lose a good friend! Everything has to be 50-50, right across the board, decisions and bills alike."

"Okay. That's the easy part."

"Another thing . . . I haven't admitted this before, but I'm not likely to be very comfortable about Billy bringing his fag friends over here. I don't choose to be around men very much, even gay men. I'm just not able to spare much energy for them or much empathy. I like Billy, but given a choice, I give my support to other women."

"So do I, most of the time. My own feminism is still developing, and I guess I'm a schmuck for vulnerability, people with needs, men included. But Billy usually doesn't bring his friends here. I see them mostly at the bars."

"Why do you go with him to the bars?"

"They're fun and exciting and I like to dance. I'm always amazed at what I see; something different and unusual happens there no matter how many times I go."

"Nothing negative?"

"What do you mean? Raids, fights? I ignore that. The bars aren't my home; neither are any of the people there."

"Then where is your home?"

"In myself, my art, one or two good friends, traveling, spending time with my mother."

"Are you looking for anything else?"

"Yeah. The right persuasion to make you relax and really want to stay here!"

"Corette, you have such a way about you! How can I resist?"

* * * * * *

Billy Acorn's return to Charleston was without fanfare. When he called Corette, there was no answer. She and Berrigan had gone to check out an ad for help at Sandy's Sub Shop. When the king of prance finally came to the apartment, attention on him was overshadowed by their own good news.

"Sham, tomorrow we don green smocks and begin our careers constructing hero sandwiches!"

"Not to mention B.L.T.'S!"

"And 'hot italians!' "

"I want one of those," Billy chimed in, trying to get in touch with the two women. But the closeness they had developed while he was gone excluded him, and he sensed it, easing out of their celebration to allow them privacy, in his attempt to be a good friend.

Through Thanksgiving and the Christmas season, Berrigan and Corette worked together for the advancement of Sandy's subs, making sandwiches until all their jeans reeked of salami and onions. Yet their enthusiasm for the job and each other remained; Berrigan was not intimidated by her parents' determined attempts to get her to come home for the holidays.

"What they really want is for me to come back to Bingham to stay. After being here, that's impossible. Unless you come with me, Corette!"

"We'll visit together, I promise. By the time we get there, maybe they'll be more mellow. Maybe for New Year's."

A thousand sandwiches behind her, a New Year's visit with Corette to Bingham approaching, and Berrigan's own feelings for Corette deepening the longer they were together: these factors served to convince Berrigan that she must let the truth surface. Rising night after night, she would walk to the railing and look down on Corette, sleeping nude on the couch, her covers kicked away in some frenzied dream.

(This is ridiculous. It isn't honest. It's got to change.)

Christmas Eve they hung stockings and went to see Billy's "new revised, redecorated rave revue" at one of the bars. Berrigan was withdrawn, steeped with the memories of Christmas past: Ju-Ju's red shawl, Syru's candlesnuffer, and with the images of St. Louis bardom in Trucker, Mac, and "The Salon." Corette was able to pull her out of her nostalgic lethargy only a little when they danced; her attentions drew Berrigan back to the present only for a moment. But in that moment, Berrigan realized how natural it was to dance with Corette. They alternated without missing a step, neither of them stopping to decide who would lead. They ended up falling over laughing when Berrigan's glasses tangled in Corette's hair, which she had brushed out and wrapped in mistletoe for the Christmas festivities. They finally limped home when the bar closed singing "White Christmas" clear up to the apartment door, and then tossing kisses to Billy from the sundeck.

They didn't stop to check their stockings, but went immediately to their beds and to sleep. About 5 A.M., Berrigan awakened, went to the bookcase where the stockings were tacked up, and looked into hers. Corette had given her a gift certificate for 17 Sandy Sub sandwiches. In the dark, she chuckled at the joke, then took the tack out of Corette's stocking.

At the couch, she looked at Corette, lying turned away from her, one breast exposed, her brown hair over her naked shoulder. The time had come for Berrigan to change the pattern of letting women come to her suggesting love. This time she could not wait to be approached, could not wait any longer for subtle signs from Corette. Time for cautious side-stepping of feelings had run out.

Berrigan touched Corette's shoulder. *"Corette? Corette?"*

The other woman rolled over, emerging from her dreams. "Berrigan?"

"Merry Christmas, Corette. My gift won't fit into your Christmas stocking, but it wears well for all seasons. It's time, Corette. Come with me. Back to your bed: to our bed."

For a moment, Corette seemed not to comprehend. But she was only letting her sleepiness subside. Then she rose from the couch, and put her arms around Berrigan. Slowly, they walked towards the loft bedroom together.

Berrigan's Journal – January 1

Day One: the really first day of happiness as person, woman, lesbian, feminist: me, Berrigan! Lying in arms warm from sleep and last night's love, we sip each other's morning breath like hope, as if the matter of heaven were here. It is, it is! It breaks like an egg that blooms a rose from its yolk. Faith rises to final lucidity whenever women sleep and love, waking to hold each other's dreams and laughter. I am on an idyll, beginning a saga of unequaled love that romantic authors would covet. "Corette, Corette, Corette" my heart keeps pulsing. Her name fills my mind and her face is a vision on all my pages.

* * * * * *

Cross country in the old jungle lion Ambassador: home to Bingham at New Year's, to bingo at the church with Dad and late-night fruit-canning with Mom. Corette won their hearts by singing "Ole Dan Tucker" to a banjo accompaniment supplied by Berrigan's grandfather, his fingers gnarled with age and his pace rickety. He laughed when the song was finished, as he had not laughed in twenty-five years, winked at Corette, touched her face and said, "Vessel of life, this girl, vessel of life."

Then the lovers went to the country with Evelyn and Daniel, built a fire at the edge of a frozen pond. Like two married couples, they sat at the fire, their shoulders touching. Berrigan looked into Evelyn's face above the orange flames, saw Daniel's hand in hers. She took Corette's hand in her own, then, snuggled closer to her, as they all passed around a flask of whiskey.

In the majestic Bingham College library, where the rule of "Hush" is paramount and strictly enforced, Berrigan offered Corette a fig newton and pointed silently, knowingly, to *Patience and Sarah,* sitting in a neutral zone under a shelf sign marked "Fiction: Rustic Adventure."

Stealing a kiss behind a stack of 1945 New York Times, the static from the rug caused them to shock each other, and their laughter peeled in cheerful prohibited echoes, cascading off the somber volumes of Johnson, Pope, Thoreau, and Dryden. Only the pages in the one slim volume of Sappho's poems were smiling at the sounds of their irreverent lesbian lark.

Snug in Berrigan's bed, Corette remarked, "Aren't you glad your parents love me? They think I'm the original Pollyana."

"Are you kidding? Don't be so smug! They love you because you brought me back to Bingham!"

The holidays ended, with a Bingham goodbye: "Come back soon, and bring Corette!" Return to Rainbow Street, New England to Dixieland, a journey into the many-fathomed montage of love and love-becoming, parents and lovers facing off over boiling fruit, knowing one another, yet unable to recognize one another.

121

"We've made the trip and now they know you, Corette. It will be all right to speak of you in my letters, often and fondly. They think we're keeping each other company, until our white knights arrive."

Chapter 8

Through the winter, the lines of moving plastic trays and workmen's faces passed in Sandy's Sub Shop. The world was a parade of anonymous hands reaching out to take sandwiches to a bored checker visciously clanging the cash register, an obnoxious clarion. But the lovers worked side by side, smiling, linked together like children by their sacred secret. All of life was compressed to concern for overlapping lettuce and ham on huge brown slices of rye, and being oblivious to the workmen and the prices and the clarion, knowing only that happy buzz of new love.

On a Tuesday morning with spring sending out magnolia scents and hanging moss glinting with remnants of night mist, with early summer beckoning boats in drydock, on a Tuesday when no sane person should use the day angrily, Berrigan and Corette were bumped from their jobs at Sandy's Sub Shop. When they arrived for the lunch shift, manager Tom Levi gave them the news.

"We're closing this shop and combining with another one in a section of town that has better business. Only a few employees here are going along."

"But what about our jobs?" Corette was frantic and angry. "What about some notice?"

Levi was unsympathetic. "What can I tell ya? Capitalism is a cruel venture. Those are the breaks."

And so on a Tuesday in May, the lovers turned in their green smocks forever, took a bus to the waterfront to walk barefoot around beercan tabs and crabs mating on the beach. They were indignant, a little shocked, and frustrated with the weak artillery they had to fight their situation.

Contemplating their renewed unemployment, Corette said, "Let's take a vacation, get away from all this craziness! Get away from sandwich shop owners whose salami is threatened by inflation!"

"But Corette, we don't have that kind of money!"

"We don't need so much. We'll panhandle or beg or steal. We could pretend to be nuns from a destitute convent. If worse comes to worst, we'll get arrested. Jail food isn't really bread and water, you know!"

"Oh Corette . . . " Berrigan flopped down in the sand, rolled on her stomach.

123

"You know you can't resist me."

Berrigan looked up into Corette's face and knew that was true.

"You're being smug again. It's really the spirit of adventure that I can't resist."

"Ah yes, the Great Unknown!"

"But thank the Goddess I know you, Corette!"

The two became sun worshippers, seeking out the private beaches around Charleston, finding little strips of white sand in front of empty waterfront houses. They had their vacation, washing off the weight of all judgments, running wildly into the surf, leaving footprints that filled up with water and faded into anonymous puddles. In the night air, at the end of a dock, they feasted on bagels and cheese, kosher pickles that dribbled cold dots of juice onto their stomachs. Their beer tabs popped with quick whooshy sounds that made the fish answer with splashes under the dock.

"I feel so illegal eating this, Corette!"

"Relax, you're a natural thief. We've got a great crime team going here. We could become legends: Bonnie and Bonnie!"

"Baloney. I caught you leaning over that deli counter. No wonder none of those guys saw me grab this stuff. They had a clear shot right down your shirtfront!"

"Power to the Breasties! Screwoggs to the Pigs!"

She lifted her shirt and wrapped it over Berrigan's head until they fell in a heap on the dock and finished the day making love while the fish answered in spashes and the old people on a houseboat watched through grey-blue night shades.

Berrigan's Journal – June 17

We are back from our vacation at the beach, back from dropping out on a reality that is inescapable. But the time, though short, was lovely and relaxing.

We sailed, letting ourselves move out over the water, letting our dreams spin and our aches dissolve. We touched minds and fingers, in between the silver sheets of wet spray that washed over us. Corette told me the water transmits something into her consciousness, a kind of unexpected recall from a time long past.

"I know we are not new lovers, Berrigan," she told me. "We've been tied together for centuries. There are memories traveling in our souls that we made together in ancient hours, probably swimming and sailing to dolphin song off the shore of Lesbos. Ours is a cosmic chemistry."

Corette, the sailing, the water, our time away from salami and strangers: these started a flow in me, and my poetry answered.

> We are lovers,
> flying "cats"
> on a restless lake.
> Other lovers

restless too, unfriendly,
bicker on their boat.
I can hear them, see them
turning away from each other
even as their sails turn
in the wind.
Storm clouds over Charleston!
The bay begins to broil
near Folly Beach.
Our sail collapses.
The voyage scuttled
behind an island,
we paddle to shore
hip deep in chilly water.

Marooned,
our cat bedraggled,
we huddle together;
lovers, friends,
wet but willing
to wait out
the throttled waves.

Unlike our sail,
our romance will never
flap pitifully in our laps,
rent by fingers of a wind
we did not choose.

Loving our love, from this vacation and from our first day
together, I try to write what I feel about it, as if to give out a script
that will reverse all the ignorance. When I read it back, I have
described a transfusion of life, a giving no word as small as coitus
can define nor a word as ugly as perversion discredit.

We come to lie together without burdened hearts, without those old rusty fears. I put my hands on your breasts,
golden globes of womanflesh that only my woman-lover
can offer. I hold them as if loaned planets of the universe
for my own pleasure. My heart sings and the flesh of you
changes, flexing with willingness. All my senses steam as
my mouth traces the curves and hollows of you, my tongue
testing each spot: ear, neck, lower back, thigh.

And what shy places bodies hide! The fawny flesh under
breasts and in the hollow of pelvic bones, backs of knees,
bends in the arm: these are new faces full of sighs that I
never met before.

When I put my mouth on your vulva, tasting the tex-
tures of Olympus (oysters, mushrooms, salty herbs), then
my soul dives into yours and I am at once entirely myself
and lost to myself. I flutter just above consciousness,

swimming in the reverie of sizzling sister-bodies loving, moving together in a sacred ballet I thought I might never learn. When you lead me in this, Corette, I know I have never danced before, nor loved so completely.

When we trade touches, taking turns in this glory, I am gone to all mundane things, belonging only to you as you move soundlessly above me, over me, through me, filling my ears with my own pulse and the rhythm of your breath.

And then when we rest, you do not leave me to silence and a cigarette or to sleep like some sated man. We lie together touching, with only just a little space between us to let the air cool the sheets and dry our sweating stomachs. We are reluctant to turn and sleep with our faces in opposite directions. In our love, there is no ritual hello-fuck-goodbye. Everything is yes-I-love-you-love-me-love-we-love, in a warm continuum of turn-taking where no one is controlled or controls. Our love has the power of powerless giving, being, coming, becoming: women, sisters, lovers, mothers, friends, souls alive at last!

Berrigan's Journal — June 25

Alas, but we must work! The pilgrimage from door to door begins again, and the frustrating search in the small print of want-ads.

I try to get Corette to linger in bed with me, resisting the call of of employment urgencies, to indulge our hot legs and tickling toes. But she will not relent and hops up and out of my arms, leaving my breasts bare to the morning chill, my eyes victim to the imposing sunlight. And what's worse, she sings! Surely there is no greater cruelty than a woman who's cheerful in the early morning!

Berrigan's Journal — June 27

Neither of us had any luck today. There is no urgent need for hurdy-gurdy grinders around town, or lady lion-tamers. The CIA is not hiring informers this week and no, thank you, the Econ-O-Lot used car dealership does not hire women. Ho hum a-holiday, unemployed are we!

Despite the glower of poverty overlooking us, we keep our good spirits. This evening Corette uncovered her paintings for me and I was again amazed at what she can do. Here are eight portraits of women: their pain, pleasure, herstory and strength, revealed in careful technique, color, and pose. She wants to do two more and possibly another five after that, so that if she gets the exhibit, she'll have 15 items to show. I am so thrilled with the first eight, I can't wait to see the next seven!

When she was chosen as a finalist for the showing, Corette submitted slides of three of these paintings of women and two slides of work she had done as art school projects. If the gallery people like the slides, she will be notified by letter. Both of us share the agony of waiting!

To ignore our present financial troubles, we made up a huge bowl of popcorn. Corette began sketching for her next two pictures and I read some poetry in a women's anthology I found on her bookshelf.

Berrigan's Journal — June 29

Corette has found work! My 5'2" mini-Amazon starts Monday as an apprentice welder for Standard Aircraft! The pay is excellent, if she can only manage to lift the welding torch! I have teased her tonight about being a baby-butch at heart, but in fact, this saves our lives, what with only peanut butter and three overripe plums in the 'fridge. By tomorrow, the plums will have puckered into three sour grimaces in the vegetable drawer. Saved from ptomaine by the Welder-Mutha!

Berrigan's Journal — July 2

The Rise and Fall of Welder-Mutha in one day: tonight I bathed my lady, rubbed her aching shoulders and salved the bites in shin and ankle left by unsisterly chunks of rough metal. Her cheeks are raw from the welding mask, her eyes numb from the white glare of the flame, her head pounding with the headache of eight factory hours listening to winches grinding and cranes dropping metal forty feet into rod-iron bins.

"Can you make it, sister?" (Your face on all my pages)
"Hold me, hold me."
"Will you be all right?" (Your chin hot against my shoulder)
"Stay with me, while I sleep."
"Sweet dreams, welder-mother (Sister-lover, little lady sore from welding airplane wings, woman, sweet, my love), sweet dreams."

Berrigan's Journal — July 23

Fortune plays a fickle game with us now; Corette's stars send her favor in large checks from Standard Aircraft, where she has become the best apprentice welder in the history of their program, with an affinity for airplane parts that borders on genius. Meanwhile, the Lady of Destiny seems perturbed with me. I landed a job painting house interiors and the same day landed at the bottom of my ladder, one foot in the paint bucket and one arm broken. So here we are, like Laurel and Hardy: Corette in her overalls leaving for the plant, lunchbox in hand, kissing me at the door (me, the Blue Cross wonder). At the bus, she turns back and gives me a wink. "See ya later, alligator!" she calls. "Screwoggs!" I answer.

She has met two women at the plant who have been helpful and sympathetic, making it easier for her to adjust to the factory atmosphere. We suspect they are also lesbians, but aren't making any assumptions at this point. I have decided that even with one hand impaired, I can still cook up a pot of spaghetti and whisk together a salad. So we're having Trudy and Jaye over for supper this week. Both of us are excited about making friends with another couple of women.

Berrigan's Journal — July 26

A day of celebration! Corette received word from the Virginia gallery that they do wish to exhibit her paintings. We spent the morning wrapping the completed canvases and then she took them off to mail on her way to work. Trudy and Jaye are coming tonight so we'll have an atmosphere of double-joy, two new ventures: in Corette's artistic career and in friendship!

Berrigan's Journal — July 27

Our spaghetti fest was great fun. Trudy brought her guitar and sang some folksongs. Then Jaye joined her to sing harmony on "Me and Bobby McGee." We all got a little drunk and started making out on the rug! When we realized there had been no declarations that we were all lesbians, it made us laugh, happy about our intuitions. They've been together four years, but have only worked at Standard Aircraft a year. They're trying to save their money to buy land in Oregon in between the mountains and the ocean.

"Y'all will have to come with us and start a women's commune," Oklahoma-born Jaye drawled. They stumbled out of here around 3 A.M., grumbling about facing airplane motors in only five hours.

Before Corette fell asleep, I told her my impressions of driving to the plant to pick her up, how it looked at night. Being with Trudy and Jaye made me think about my impressions all the more, since they spoke so often of the plant and their work.

"You should paint the plant, Corette, and include it in your series for the gallery. All those rotund smoke stacks, some of them pooching on one side or the other, some of them leaning, all of them belching blasts of steam simultaneously. Your paints could catch the lights: blue, white, silver, and yellow. You've been working so hard since you started welding! Please take a break and paint. It always brings you back in touch with things."

Her answer was muffled, on the edge of sleep. "I want to paint the women on the *inside* of the plant. But I'll paint again soon, I promise."

Berrigan's Journal — July 29

What a day at sea! With just the wind sailors dream of, the wind that carries siren song and fills our sail like a proud bosom! I am losing my landlubber's clumsiness enough to enjoy the orgasmic thrill of straddling a cat-deck, and lifting one sleek runner out of the water.

We fly across Poseidon's back, dipping and falling into the

troughs over the swells, appearing and disappearing on the surface, so dazzling that I lose my senses and think I'm gliding on some vast acrylic sculpture! It could only be better if we could fly a hull and make love at the same time! (Corette was dear; she wrapped my cast in a plastic bag.)

Berrigan's Journal — August 5

Corette went out on the patio early this morning and began painting. She came in only once during the day, to get some "art muck:" shreds of lettuce, raw garbanzos and artichokes. Later she put a concerto on the stereo and stroked her canvas as though the brush were a conductor's wand. When she finished, exhausted, she slumped onto the couch and I got her a bowl of fruit and some wine.

"Show it to me!"

"No. I want you to look at what I've painted alone, and write a poem for what you see there. My picture will feel empty without a poem from you as companion."

So evolves our second artistic collaboration. Corette worked on four canvases, but only completed one, a picture of the plant done in abstract, swirls of color, the paint alternately thick and thin, bright and dull, the movement of the industry kinetic, yet momentarily frozen. And out of this chaos of suggested movement are focal points: not the lights or the smokestacks, not the silver bellies of planes or the petal-like rotors. She has concentrated on the faces of women, straining, and their hard red arms, lifting, welding: women birthing weightless sky creatures out of rusty steel.

Confined to tight skinny stanzas, like Trudy's skinny ass and Jaye's tight strong arms (they seem specks of lavender surprise in the grey blasé of airplane parts), I add to the painting my poem.

> Sister,
> blueshirted sister,
> standing
> toiling
> just down the line,
> winding wires
> for 707 rotors,
> Sister,
> you do that good.
> Better than
> most of the men,
> Better than
> some of the
> other sisters.
> Yeah,
> you do it
> good.
> Sister,
> welding

with sparks
and flame,
riveting
small bolts
from your
hand-gun,
Sister,
making jets
that don't fall
from the sky,
you do that good.
Better than
most of the men,
Better than
some of the
other sisters.
Yeah,
you do it good.

And Sister,
when you love me,
with your
blue shirt
pulled off
your naked shoulders,
you do that good.
Better than
any man.
Better than
the other sisters.
Yeah,
you do it good.
You weld me
to you
and we fly
on wings
and dreams
more glorious
than silver jets.

Berrigan's Journal — August 20
　　Unable to work, barely capable of simple cooking (except salad and spaghetti), my broken arm could easily send me into a depression. But Luck at least spared me my writing hand so I am not separated from my poetry. And when I grow weary of writing, I read the poetry other women have written. It gives me goosebumps, this legacy of words we leave each other.
　　But in truth, the recent poetry I've read and written has been only an addition to Corette's attentions in staving off my feelings of

inadequacy (that I cannot contribute to our income, that I have become a self-pitying invalid, that I might appear to be "cashing in" on our relationship, that I am subjecting her to playing a "butch" role). Her patience is unending, her supplications to my comfort constant. She calls me on every break at the plant, always with a new joke, a cheery "I love you; how ya doing', alligator?" Sometimes she puts Jaye or Trudy on the line too. She's started telling me stories, creating wild colorful fantasies as brilliant as her paintings. They come to me over the Bell in delightful installments.

At night after Corette has finished painting, we talk and exchange fantasies. We relive those most recent pasts that we did not share. While this cannot embellish what we know of each other already, it is stimulating entertainment to recall our former days. We practice our sense of humor on each other and our greatest oratory.

Corette has been keeping an incredible pace lately, though, and I worry about her. Besides diligently nursing me, and working to the point of exhaustion on the planes, she paints several hours every night, determined to finish those other seven canvases to send to Virginia.

She is not as easy-going as I first thought, or else becoming a welder has made her stubborn! She resists all my efforts to get her to rest. The series of paintings is coming along well, but she won't let me see them. "Artistic privilege," she tells me!

Berrigan's Journal – August 27
Since I will be getting this cast off in about ten days, Jaye and Trudy came by to prepare it properly. With lavender marking pens, they turned the cast into a work of erotic art, drawing stick-figure women in kama-sutra couplings and giving vent to the most blatant sapphic graffiti. Naturally, no names were signed but they volunteered to accompany me for the removal ceremony just to see what the doctor would say!

Berrigan's Journal – September 3
At 5:15 the door burst open and Corette came in with two squirmy puppies, one under each arm. Flushed with the effort of containing them, and seeing my surprise, she launched into a non-stop defense:

"A guy at work had too many and he said he was going to drown them! I couldn't let that happen, could I? And besides, this kind of dog makes a great house pet and watchdog. They're free . . . and it's partly a celebration too! Of you getting the cast off! You can strengthen your muscles in that hand by leash-training the puppies!"

(Here one of them took a delicate dump on my shoe.)
"Looks like leash-training isn't all they need!"
"Screwoggs! After all Berrigan, we can't let all those psycholo-

131

gists down, can we? All those learned men of science who've written all those books about the many neuroses of lesbians! We have to help them prove that every good lesbian couple needs pets, as child substitutes!"

Before she could sputter any more of her half-logic, which was most amusing to me (though I couldn't let her know!), I said, *"I'm not buying one bit of any of that, Corette. They sure as hell aren't housebroken."*

The other pup had now followed suit with the first. Corette's eyes fell. I leaned down and let one of the pups crawl into my sling, resting on the cast where it started licking my fingers. Corette looked at me more hopefully. I had come to the end of my ability to pretend frowns and skepticism about the pups. As the one I held grew warm against me, I asked my lover, *"Well, what shall we name them?"*

Berrigan's Journal — September 9

"C. Day:" the cast comes off, letting out into the air a grey flaky lump of fingers: stiff, sore, slightly creaky at first use. Somewhat sadly I bid farewell to my plaster glove immortalized with lavender lyrics.

In celebration, we bought ice cream cones and let the dogs lick them: the coldness on my hand felt strange, as the nerves have been lazy for nearly six weeks. Then we went down to the beach, where the dogs barked at the rolling waves, running out of the water and shaking their paws in bewilderment. Every few minutes they came back to where we were sitting, ran in circles around us, pushing their noses against us to leave salty splotches on our jeans. Paloma and Hoby, we call them, little creatures on spindly legs who nearly burst with life and zest for exploring.

When we got back to the apartment, I walked in to find everything decorated in toilet paper, and a big banner hung in the living room reading, "Welcome Back, Superfingers!" Jaye and Trudy popped up over the bedroom railing, giggling, wearing lavender clown-hats.

I left most of the memory of the rest of the evening behind me in two or three bottles of wine. But the final celebration came in private moments with Corette, not only for the removal of the cast, and the new pups, but for our both surviving to find each other in a world where it is often unsafe for alive-and-well women to walk the streets.

> shivers of sun
> through dandelion hair
> are like the tendril'd touches
> we share.
>
> bright and rapt
> we fall, embracing,
> women's love

and legs enlacing,
leaving lines of sighs
as tracing,
of our touches,
eager spent.

I have risen to write this poem while Corette sleeps (not as she used to, on the couch below me with her white breasts beyond my touch). After she loved me, held me, and finally left me reluctantly, turning asleep, unknowing that her sleep mapped her in a different direction, I lay awake listening to us breathe. Hanging my unbound arm over the edge of the bed, I stroked the pups. They sigh and mutter in their own dreams, twitching, running in some dog's adventure. But how soft and vulnerable their plump upturned bellies, white and warm and trusting of my touch: like Corette's breast, the sanctuary of my dreams.

Berrigan's Journal — September 10
Corette and I have been busy for the last week drawing up blue-prints for a minor carpentry project in the apartment: changing the ladder up to the loft into a short staircase. Corette wants to do most of the work; she's worried my arm isn't up to hammering and sawing. I am, of course, stubbornly denying that!

We've got the conversion all designed now and are going to shop for nails, plywood, paint, and last but not least, overalls! It's too bad Evelyn isn't here to help; I'm sure she'd feel like Rebecca of Sunnybrook Farm in a pair of overalls with paint on her Hartford-proper nose!

Berrigan's Journal — September 12
Our staircase is progressing rapidly. Corette is an adept builder and very patient with me as I hammer in half my nails bent. I'm the expert on the saw, though, and it's good exercise to strengthen the arm. Paloma and Hoby lay near our feet, sneezing from the saw dust and chewing the hammer handle.

Berrigan's Journal — September 14
We have nearly finished the staircase. All it lacks is a coat of paint. We are proud of our labors; it's sturdy and all the edges fit tight and smooth. But the clean-up may be more difficult than the building! I suggested training the pups to use a whisk broom but so far all they do is spread wood scraps everywhere and look up at me innocently.

* * * * * *

The agonized waiting about Corette's paintings ended in mid-September with an unexpected letter from the Virginia gallery. Berrigan called Corette at work and she raced home over her lunch hour to tear into the envelope.

133

"What does it say? What does it say! Tell me!"

Corette read the letter silently, moving her mouth to form the words, with an expression of disbelief that Berrigan couldn't decipher as joy or bewilderment.

"I don't believe it," Corette said, dropping the letter on the couch and walking out onto the porch, leaving Berrigan with no news except her back and the screen door slamming. Berrigan picked up the letter and read it, unprepared for its contents.

"We must retract our agreement to show your paintings," it began. "From the slides we were unable to gauge that all the canvases were poses of women." It went on. "The theme is too singular, not universal enough." And then the clincher: "These portraits show obvious artistic talent but are possibly political enough to offend some buyers. We must respect the tastes of our regular patrons."

Berrigan approached Corette, who was holding onto the porch railing and shaking with anger.

"Damn, damn, damn!" Corette cried, hitting the railing with her fists. Berrigan put her arms around Corette, using her body to buffer the sobs. Slowly they sank onto the porch together, rocking back and forth until the anger subsided and the afternoon faded into evening.

Later that night, Corette phoned her mother and they exchanged a strong but tearful conversation.

"I have some news we both knew but must have forgotten somewhere along the way. Only men in art are universal! I'm starting my own art form, Mother. The non-happening. It's an exhibition you announce with no intentions of it's ever really occurring!"

Berrigan's Journal – September 28

Since she called her mother, Corette has not mentioned the paintings. She has more anger still to let out, but holds it inside herself now. I tried to talk to her, telling her that creating the portraits was the work of art. Their worth is not invalidated because one gallery is too short-sighted to show them. But she is not relieved by that and asks that we not discuss it anymore. I am trying to respect her desire to mend herself, but am also stymied in trying to comfort her. She has a stubborn streak! I have realized through her reaction to this incident that I may have taken Corette's strength for granted. She always seems to be so well equipped to handle everything; I feel foolish that I have done her this disservice by not remembering that her emotions are as sensitive as mine.

* * * * * *

In early October, ripe circumstances netted Berrigan a job in the infirmary at Standard Aircraft and so the foursome (Berrigan,

Corette, Jaye, Trudy) grew closer. Gradually Berrigan and Corette were pulled into the dream of the Oregon commune: an escape into nature, a step towards a womanculture with clay beadwork on the wall, planting and harvesting, woman's life into the life of the land. All of it seemed to move in a circle of birthing with no harsh right-angles, no erections to leave marks in the process. They were sisters, loving, women supporting each other, looking towards a reachable dream. Corette had not painted since September, immersing herself into Oregon planning instead of her art, taking solace in a new dream to avoid dealing with her own shattered one.

For several months, they chattered in avid plan-making, between the hours of winding gauze bandages, welding metal-to-metal, and riveting rotors on the silver noses of jets. At the apartment, they played poker and sang to Trudy's guitar. They shared Christmas dinner together, briefly dropping in on Billy's latest club act. Berrigan called Evelyn; she had just become officially engaged to Daniel. Late Christmas night, just before they went to bed, Berrigan asked Corette for a very special present.

"Finish the portrait series. That would be your best gift to me."

After Christmas came and went, when the wreaths were taken off the doors, after winter blew in and out without hurricanes, Spring came with April in Charleston, gleaming in the moss and the joyous streaks of the dogs leaping out of puppyhood. Corette knew then that she could not leave the South for Oregon. She had found so much love in Charleston, found herself time and time again in sailing, in touching her primal memory on those waters. It was not at the border of Vermont, her mother's land, where the countryside told her "You are home." That message came to her only when she reached Charleston.

"My roots are here," she explained to the disappointed friends. "I grew into myself and my love with my lady here. It's comfortable. Not the challenge of your dream, perhaps, but I know a calm here that is too dear to leave just yet. Save us a space in your Oregon home, though. We will come eventually."

"No one bakes bread as good as you do, Corette," Jaye told her, and the tears ran down one cheek. They hugged and held each other. Trudy took a twang on her guitar and howled like a hound-dog and they all laughed away some of the immediate sorrow. None of the dream was really lost, only just shaken a little in that it would not be immediately shared.

Corette soon found an additional reason to stay in Charleston. Her friend Dee called to tell her about a used catamaran for sale. A man who worked for an oil company was being transferred to California and decided to liquidate some of his property, including the boat. It was in first-rate condition. The money they had saved for the Oregon property would make a down-payment. The deal was good as soon as Berrigan would co-sign the loan at the bank; then they would become the proud owners of the 16-foot boat,

"Fireseed," its colors blue and white. But before Berrigan had a chance to finalize the papers, Jaye and Trudy found a piece of land in Oregon and needed a ride to Atlanta to catch their plane.

The man who owned the sailboat agreed to hold the deal until they could get back from Atlanta. Excited by the near-achievement of their separate dreams, yet still loving in a special togetherness, the four of them drove to Atlanta, singing "Me and Bobby McGee" most of the way, taking frequent stops to look at the scenery. The last remnants of winter were slowly undressing into nubile spring. The dogs ran stretching out their muscles in the brisk air, running with an ease, their muzzles smiling in the puddles where they drank. At one stop, the four women joined hands and danced in a slow circle, singing soft tunes, unmatching yet overlapping fond melodies. They stopped and listened and heard their own emotions meet in the harmony. Then came the tears and laughter of willing pain, the bearable pain of parting when sisters do not say "Goodbye" but "See ya soon! Have a good life!"

Berrigan leaned her head against the cool glass window, watching the jet that carried Jaye and Trudy to their nature retreat, their dream land in Oregon.

"See you later, alligators," she mumbled.

The jet lifted its silver chin up over the trees at the end of the runway, dipped each wing side to side, and then arched towards a spot in the sky, up and out of sight. Berrigan looked at Corette, looked at the back of her lover's head, and wanted to touch her hair. Turning as if hearing this silent wish, Corette said, "I hope that's one of the planes we made."

Spinning wheels: Corette's old car going clunkety-clunkety out of Atlanta back towards Charleston. Spinning tales: Corettes' voice surging up and down, low then loud, through the adventurous tones of laughter and imitation, manufacturing fantasy and fiction to burn away the road and memory. Driving, singing, listening to the fading echo of "Bobby McGee" went these lovers, spinning time into bindings, leaving unspoken the tears behind their thoughts for the friends just departed.

On the other side of Augusta, Paloma stood up in the back seat and put her nose against Berrigan's shoulder.

"I think we need to pull over, Corette. I'm getting a rest stop signal!"

In the late-April sunshine, Berrigan watched her family play: Corette running with the dogs, tripping, laughing, her breasts lolling to and fro inside her velour shirt. It was as if Corette herself contained the season of spring, kicking up its heels.

(Boogie mama and the boogie babies: dogs of a lesbian and the lesbian herself, crazy, dancing in the April sun. Thank Goddess, I am here to see them!)

Paloma loped around Corette in circles. Hoby ran at her legs, bumping her, barking. Berrigan clapped her hands, *"Here dogs, here dogs!"* They raced off towards her, smothering her in wet hellos. And when the dogs were winded, they lay with all four feet stretched out in the sun, licking afternoon moisture off the grass. The lovers,without audience, welcomed Spring as She edged over the Earth, gliding at the horizon like a lover leave-taking.

Home again, and inquiring about the boat, Corette and Berrigan learned that the man selling it had gone to the West Coast to find a house, but would be back in May. His wife told them he would definitely sell them the boat, and they could finalize the deal upon his return. Corette was vexed at having to wait another several weeks. She was so excited about owning her own boat that to have the deal impending was agony, even with a verbal agreement.

"Relax," Berrigan told her, *"there won't be any good sailing until July anyway."*

Waiting for the boat deal to come through and still dosed with the sorrow of Trudy and Jaye's departure, both women were restless and distracted. Berrigan tried to write and was blocked; at one point she threw her thesaurus across the room in frustration. Corette paced and fidgeted, went from TV to music to trying to read. Berrigan hoped she might go to her painting, but Corette resisted. She finally gave in, although her first attempt was aborted as she stomped into the house, bemoaning, "All my brushes are fraying!"

Corette tried again to paint several evenings later but couldn't keep her attention on the work. On the third try, she went out onto the back porch and didn't return for several hours. Encouraged, Berrigan was about to go out and see if Corette had started again on finishing her portrait series when she heard loud noises.

Running to see what was happening, Berrigan found Corette smashing a canvas and frame against the railing of the porch. The picture was of a male nude she had painted in school. Now she was angrily destroying it.

Before Berrigan could say anything, Corette flung the tattered picture out over the porch and watched it clatter to the ground. She turned back to Berrigan, hearing her at the door.

"I'm blocked! I can't get started again! I've tried to sketch and nothing comes! You see what I've let them do to me with their rejection? I'm at a distance from myself, my art, my . . ."

"Let me hold you. It will be all right."

Berrigan took a step towards her lover, but Corette pushed her arm, pushed her away.

"I don't want you to hold me! There is no comfort in the world for me at this moment! My paintings aren't being shown. They're covered up, forgotten! Trudy and Jaye have left us. I hate those fucking airplanes, and there's hair in the sink! The laundry isn't done and women in India are starving! There's bugs in the basement! Nothing is ever going to be all right again! Never! Never!"

Corette was stamping her feet and flinging her brushes all over the porch. She stopped just short of toppling her potters wheel and a table full of small sculptures. Berrigan sat down on the doorstep to watch this tantrum, holding her chin in her hand. They contemplated each other. Berrigan put her hand out again, and Corette came and sat in her arms and they laughed and cried and cussed the world together.

"Now, want to come with me and clean the sink? We'll wash all our cares and hairs right down the drain!"

* * * * * *

Finally about to make the last arrangements to buy the catamaran, Berrigan was finishing a letter to Trudy and Jaye at work before she took off early from the plant to go to the bank. Corette had taken the day off and was with the man from California, inspecting the "Fireseed." He did not need to be at the bank to witness Berrigan's signature on the loan.

Several days earlier, Corette had told Berrigan she wanted to take the boat for a trial run before they signed the final papers. Berrigan tried to veto this.

"There isn't any place safe to sail yet. The water's rough everywhere. Besides, you'd catch your death of cold! If I have anything to say about this, it's a firm NO! You don't want to jeapordize your potential to live to be 106 as the oldest lady-welder, do you?"

The tone of Berrigan's disapproval was light, but her concern about Corette going out sailing too soon was obvious. Corette only half-conceded. "I promise I'll use good sense."

Stopping at home on the way to the bank, Berrigan put the letter to Trudy and Jaye in the mail. Just before she went out the door, she checked the kitchen table in case Corette had left her a note. There was a package there with Berrigan's name on it, which she opened. In it was a small blue dish, covered with laminated butterfly wings. It had a note attached:

> "Saw this yesterday and somehow thought you would understand it. It is at once beautiful and tragic, rather like us at times, like all woman-lovers: trapped in their flight for freedom. I love you.
>
> Corette
>
> P.S. Billy is coming over later to cook us a 'soul-food' supper. Please leave the back door unlocked."

An hour later, having traversed the erratic zip-zip of freeway maniacs lost with their bearings berserk, Berrigan conquered the downtown traffic and reached the bank. It took another forty minutes to locate the proper clerk, files and papers, and the attention of a bank official.

138

Berrigan had just inked her signature on the loan when the phone on the clerk's desk buzzed. "It's for you," he said, handing her the receiver.

"Hello."

"Berrigan? It's Billy. Can you come home immediately?"

"What's up? You sound terrible! Don't tell me you burned the chitluns!"

"No . . . it's Corette. There's been . . . an accident. She . . . they took the boat out. I guess the water was pretty rough. They got out too far, and coming around, the boom hit her."

"Where is she? Is she at a hospital? How badly is she hurt?"

"No, she's . . . Berrigan, she drowned. They're looking for the body now."

Berrigan's Journal — June 25

I cannot cry any more, unless I could weep my own blood. It seems that I have let out tears enough to match those depths of water which covered Corette today. There is no one to hold me and tell me this has not happened, is not so. To write is the only relief I can think of; I am calmer now, so I can write. But the pain is so close!

When I got the news from Billy, I rushed out into the street. All the buildings telescoped out of view, wobbling. I thought they might topple on me. They all grew eyes and leaned over to look at me, voyeurs into my grief. The brakes on a bus spit a funereal spear through me: *Corette is dead.* The people on the streets grew ugly. They all looked huge-headed, with bulbous hungry eyes. Panic made me breathless. I thought all at once that the lame cats had formed a pack to tear me to pieces.

Then a car bumped a post and I jolted; my heart stopped. It was as if I had heard the boom swing around and strike Corette.

Where is solace when your gay lover dies? The bars? Full of cliques of cowboys, hippies, old dykes, flashy partners, desperate loners? No, not there, where a friend of Billy's once stared into the darkness and said, "Dead birds. This place is full of dead birds." Death has its bastion there already, having exiled sympathy and hope long ago.

Where then? Home? To people who cannot even perceive me, much less my love and loss? To friends? Those who also mourn Corette and are beyond even huddling with me to sob in unison?

My isolation in our "us" has built a wailing wall between myself and the reach of others and any shared consolation or comfort. So I am at the wall of my creation, chanting out my grief upon the akashic fabric, trying in vain to reach through the tissue of the universe and touch Corette.

Chapter 9

On the plane to Vermont, a plane with a casket in its cargo, Berrigan's mourning the loss of her lover began a dark mood, isolating her in a space empty and hurting with loneliness. She leaned her forehead against the window.

(The land lies in a patchwork below me, weaving a fine pattern across the states. I'm a fool in an airplane that hangs in the sky. Defying all reason, we do not crash, do not fall like a fireball of metal and burning bodies into the quilt below with its red and green squares. Instead we put our faith and trust and dead lovers out on the surface of air, hoping jet engines and the god-technology will prevail. Some of us pray and some of us sleep in the roar of speed against a steel shell, and some of us recite a karmic rosary.

Airplanes: tons of steel and noise that carry friends and dreams and lovers away from each other, or towards burial: airplanes that should crash but fly instead, which my lover may have welded together. Corette and I used to go sit on a construction site near the airport in Charleston. Night after night, we watched planes launching out of a necklace of blue runway lights. With my hand in Corette's, nothing was impossible.

The plane touches clouds. In fairy tales, clouds are the homes of dreams. What have my dreams brought me? From the books Adrienne Dulcea put in my hands to the dreams that spoke to me out of Corette's paintings: what is left of my life but a dream now drowned, swallowed up and laid on satin pillows in a coffin? My songs have gone underwater and I cannot hear them anymore.)

Relatives of Corette's whom Berrigan had not met were already at Corral Pablo when she arrived. The gentleman handling most of the arrangements was obviously Captain Jack. He was cordial, warm, and most of all, efficient at a difficult time for ValJean. Berrigan and ValJean embraced briefly, holding each other, taking away some of the shakes and the terror of aloneness.

"I've given you a room with lots of windows," ValJean told Berrigan. "There are several telegrams for you on the nightstand. Billy will be here tonight."

"She's not to be buried in Charleston?"

"No. Here, in the plot next to her father, on the edge of this property."

Later, when many of the guests had gone to the church for the wake, Berrigan went into her room, put on a terrycloth robe and sat on the bed.

140

(Buried here? Her roots are in Charleston. She said so herself, many times. Who took her choice away? She's going to be buried next to her father. Why not on the shore where the sailboats pass, where her woman-lover lives? Where have all the choices and dreams and lovers gone?)

There were two telegrams on the bedside table. The first was from Evelyn, telling Berrigan to call or come and stay with her. "Daniel will vacate to give us time," the message said in closing.

The second telegram was unexpected, a shock.

"Talking to Evelyn, I learned of your loss. I am very sorry. If I can be of any help, or if you need me, please be sure to call." It was sent by Linda Framer.

Berrigan undressed and got into bed, turning her face to the wall, feeling her breasts cold against the sheets.

(I'm sorry, Corette, for not attending your wake, for wondering why there is no choice to your final resting next to a man's grave, even your father's. But I want to remember you always as you were to me: full of laughter and adventure. I wished we could die and be buried together so that our loving, our togetherness, would never end, nor our spell be broken by any parting. Even in death we would have loved. Forgive me, but you understand my selfishness. I won't embarass anyone, but I won't deny how I loved you. Goodnight. I am so used to telling you goodnight, so un-used to sleeping cold and alone in a bed. Goodnight, my love.)

Berrigan dozed, then awoke suddenly, feeling an unusual warmth along one side of the bed and covers, along her backside, a warmth she often felt when sleeping with Corette. The covers were warm to the touch, as if in answer, as if Corette wanted to tell Berrigan she was with her even buried so far from Charleston, even in an empty bed.

"Corette," Berrigan whispered into the darkness. *"Corette?"*

Flapping in a June Vermont gust, one of the four ropes holding the canopy over the family had to be secured by a man from the funeral home. The minister paused in his eulogy until this was done. His hair was blown wild by the wind, and he kept flicking it out of his eyes. Captain Jack and Billy flanked ValJean to block the wind and support her. Berrigan stood to Billy's right; there were just the four of them on the first row under the canopy, directly in front of the long silver casket. The rest of Corette's relatives sat behind them. Berrigan could not see ValJean's face beneath a dark net. She could not see Corette's face beneath the metal lid, sealed and bound away forever. She could only see Billy's profile, and Captain Jack occasionally nodding and turning his face in towards ValJean.

(What does he say to her? What can a man possibly say to a woman full of grief? "Come let me hold you"? "It will be all right"? "I am with you"?)

"Remember if you can," the minister concluded, his black robe

141

whipping at his knees, "that Death is Celebration. The spirit of this girl whom we loved has gone to Paradise, to live in Eternal Grace with her Master, our Lord Jesus Christ."

(I defy you! I did not owe you Corette: for paradise, eternal masters, or male faces not covered by nets!)

Each in turn of the family and friends walked from their places under the canopy, dropping a handful of dirt onto the casket as it slowly lowered into the grave on an automatic bier. Captain Jack arranged a 10-gun salute since Corette was a member of a military family. The guardsmen were completely out of place in misfitting uniforms and badly adjusted equipment. People were filing out towards their cars. ValJean stumbled against Billy. Berrigan gasped, desperate to run back to that hole in the ground and haul Corette back up into the air. One of the officers gave the command and all ten guns went up onto the shoulders of all ten men in one tinny clink. Then the rounds went off one at a time in huge explosions, each gun finishing with a breath of powder.

(Why are guns fired at funerals? Are they the voice of death?)

The minister stepped up to ValJean, took her hand and spoke softly to her. Berrigan was at the edge of the dispersing crowd, still holding her handful of dirt. Weaving slightly as the wind buffeted her, she watched the people. There was ValJean, leaning against a man in black, his hair wild, his face uncovered. Billy and Captain Jack, waiting to one side, lit a cigarette. The Captain put his hand on Billy's arm. At their cars behind her, the honor guardsmen put their guns in the trunks. The trunks came down loudly and Berrigan shuddered. One of the men laughed; the sound jolted her.

"I wasn't sure my piece would fire," he said.

Then the hearse drove up. Billy, Captain Jack, and ValJean got in for the return to the studio. They slid away in that long black car that was too shiny to take death seriously. And Berrigan was finally alone at the edge of the hole, looking down on the casket partially covered with dirt. She raised her hand up high and let the dirt fall slowly. The minister folded his robes and watched her, wondering who she was, this last woman staring into the grave. Was she crazy?

(Life goes on from the moment our dreams expire with our bodies, even at the hour of our burial. Life goes on, new life begins. Does death sow all the seeds? Time sheds us so easily, in words and tears and silver boxes. The present rushes on without backward glancing, around us grieving. But I cannot go on like death and life, without backward glancing, without looking for you, Corette, whose face has been on all my pages, against my cheek in sleep, against my heart and hands in loving. I report now in promises and prayers; there will never be enough tears, enough wreaths, enough memories, enough silent shudders and invisible sobs to say for all years remaining how I love you, how I miss you.)

"Do you want a ride back to town with me?" the minister

interrupted.

"No. I'll walk."

"In this wind?"

"I'll walk."

(Leave me alone, man, ungrieving, your face uncovered, here where my lover is buried. What scriptures would you quote me if you knew "this girl whom we loved" was my love, my woman-lover? The only "celebration" in eulogies are for those of us so selfishly glad not to be in silver coffins.)

"I'm driving back today. You're welcome to come along," Billy told Berrigan.

(June 29, Corette dead four days.)

"I think I'd be better off on a plane full of strangers."

"I'm not asking you to be good company."

"All right."

ValJean did not stand at the gate of Corral Pablo for this departure, as she had upon Berrigan's first visit. In fact, she only saw them a few moments to say goodbye. She had remained secluded since the funeral, even from Captain Jack. Billy and Berrigan walked through her studio on their way out; Ned and Chip were in the livingroom, lying still and unanimated, all their excited barking quieted. It was as if they perceived the mood of the household. Berrigan looked into the dark garage where ValJean painted. The shapes of the covered canvases, sawhorses, and easels were muted in the blackness. Suspended without light, the life of her paintings was elusive, just as the adventurous mind and creative brushes of Corette were now forever still.

On the trip returning to Charleston, there was little conversation between Berrigan and Billy, but neither of them expected it. At one point, Billy pulled off the road to stretch his legs, while Berrigan walked out into some trees near the road. There the image of that afternoon near Augusta came back to her, painful at first, tears stinging her eyes. Then it mellowed and she let the memory redraw itself: different territory, different time, but the lady the same: special, singular. She could envision Corette running with the dogs, the spirit of Spring embodied in her, kicking up its heels. Berrigan picked up some of the loose red earth and thought immediately of that handful she had dropped onto the casket in Vermont. Then the picture of the dogs and Corette's joyfulness with them came back, loaning Berrigan a long-absent smile. She returned to the car, saying to herself out of this mental retreat, *"Boogie mama and the boogie babies."* Once in the car, she wrote in her notebook:

"Earth, earth: Georgia earth once held our sighs. Vermont earth now holds you in a cold womb. And this Earth where I remain alone runs through my fingers. But it is you, my lady, my love, Corette, who falls away from me, runs

143

through my fingers like loose earth, like dreams that crumble and smell of sod."

Berrigan's Journal — July 2

When Billy left, I stood at the open door of the apartment, and I didn't know if I could go in. There is so much of Corette here. I finally crossed to the screened porch and let out the dogs, who have been cared for by a neighbor. The din of their welcome-home barking was too much for me, so I sent them out to the yard. Still in my coat, suitcase packed by the door as though I were only a visitor, I walked numb through the entire apartment. Staring at all these familiar objects we bought and made together, touching them, my tired mind formed a question behind aching eyes: *"Why? Why Corette? Why not Jaye or Trudy or Syru or Billy or Mac or Stager or my father's favorite nephew or Robin Daltry? Why? Why Corette?"*

Out on the porch where Corette did all her painting, I found a sketchbook of her failed attempts at my portrait. "Screwoggs!" she finally penciled over one of them. She had a good start in clay on two female figures. Sitting upon the turntable, the half-formed figures poised for a dance which will never have music.

There are several letters here that came while I was in Vermont: one from my parents, two from Jaye and Trudy. How can I read them when I can't begin to conceive of a way to answer?

Berrigan's Journal — July 7

Has it been five days since I last wrote in this journal? The hours pass me while I am either pacing, or sitting turning the pages of the sketchbook. I have looked at each drawing over and over again: they are Corette's love letters. She drew a lot of new female poses recently. All the hips and nipples, all the curves and points, eventually reach upwards, like woman-hands grabbing for the sky.

Berrigan's Journal — July 10

The phone rang and rang this morning. Something in me doesn't care who's calling. I don't have anything to say to anyone. I took the receiver off the hook until I was afraid the phone company might come to see what's wrong. So I dial Time-and-Temperature, a movie-house recording, even Dial-A-Prayer, and just let them keep repeating. I don't have the energy to get a repairman to disconnect it. What would I say when he came to the door?

"I don't need this phone anymore. My lover's dead, you see, and so there's no one I care to talk to."

More mail — strange addresses on little white envelopes the size of party invitations. They're probably consolation notes from friends who haven't written in years.

Berrigan's Journal — July 13

I dreamed the "Please Accept Our Sympathy" cards were making a noise in the bowl where they sit by the door . . . cheeping noises, like chicks chipping out of eggs. Then they poured out of a bag and smothered me.

Another letter came today from my parents. What kind of a noise will it make in my dreams?

Berrigan's Journal — July 20

Billy came by; I saw his car from the porch. I didn't answer the door, even though he knows I'm here. But what can we give each other? Hands full of grief pushing an unspeakable burden back and forth between us? When he leaves, we're both still carrying the same burden, the same pain.

Berrigan's Journal — August 4

I spent today soul-searching, looking at the death of Corette, of us, of myself, lying around me in pitiful wounded pieces. It's all unresurrectable, yet unburyable: that partnership, and my old self. My former dreams smoulder, like a cruel ember, a fire eye of me looking at myself. I wish I could celebrate, go on valiantly, but I'm still a grave within myself, gaping at the yawning emptiness of love's leaving so violently. I'm not the full-blown woman-lover Corette deserved. She would abhore this desertion of my own goals, this lazy mourning. For her sake, I should wear an ash cross on my forehead to let my reflections know it is time for a metamorphosis out of grief and into reality. But when the fragile cocoon of my soul is shaken loose, what if the butterfly lies dead inside? What if my poetry has gone on sabbatical and fallen into Pompeii's ruins?

Berrigan's Journal — August 10

I am shattering without interest in my own dissolution, watching chunks of me dance past under a strawhat, with a cane accompaniment going "pitty pat, pitty pat." Where is all that renowned strength all my whiz-kid friends said I had? What I am in substance is all shattering, busting into pieces of dust, leaving me a humorless no-person shell. Evelyn and Doris and Corette would be ashamed to see me like this. But who ever made the rule that says you have to keep on trying? And who ever tried to teach me how to be a brave warrior?

Berrigan's Journal — August 13

The spines of poems rattle around in my head like old bones with broken edges, skeletons that do not have all their parts. Some of the moving joints are missing, still unearthed from their mysterious graves in my soul.

Berrigan's Journal — August 21

Here are my ramblings, written while the laundry is in the dryer: Corette's clothes and mine spinning round and round. Shouldn't I pack her away with a clean memory?

In the fog that has become my life, all perimeters unclear, a starship's run aground, its sails shredded, bow buckled, clearly flying the flag of distress.

145

Round and round the World she runs
stumbling, and I wander
inside a pinball machine, striking people like scoring colored lights.

I become a split-image, striking, being struck, my score stuck on TILT.

Panting, parting, who paints the portrait of a butterfly in pipe dreams, who talks and tries to do, against the colored lights, ending up a vague faded fisted tatoo? Corette? Corette? Corette!
Bojangles girl in spangles: is this me?
Woman starship run aground,
a breast in distress
alone at night against the sheets: is this me?
Clownface for the people! Pretend that Death is Celebration!
To retrieve me, I will take my poems into the brain from whence they sprang, waiting for the time when I can write again, when they will come home to me like lost children returned from hoary woods. But when will they come home? Or did all the poems drown too?

Berrigan's Journal — September 5
For weeks, I haven't slept. I awaken in the terror of recurring nightmares. I am underwater. Bubbles trail out behind me as I move. I hear a grating sound. I turn in the water, unable to see anything or locate the sound. I struggle through endless acres of seaweed which clings to me. I am afraid of the kelp, afraid it will strangle me, cover my head like the suffocating bag of sympathy cards in my other dreams.

Suddenly the grass parts to reveal a cave with four bars across its entry. Corette is behind the bars: she pulls at them. This is the grating noise. I motion to her but I cannot seem to approach any closer. When she sees me, she puts her hands through the bars and beckons me, mournfully. Her cries are strange underwater sounds: unbearable, pitiful, beseeching. I cannot move towards her, and the cave begins to move farther and farther away from me, until the kelp closes again and I cannot see Corette anymore. All the scene becomes invisible then, in a panicked rush of bubbles. I awaken, panicked, as if *I* am drowned. Yet it is not a fear of death that causes the terror but that I am not reunited with Corette, as if she isn't really dead at all, but unjustly stolen from me forever. I ache with the fear that someone has played a cruel joke on me.

Berrigan's Journal — September 11
The nightmares continue, unabated. Desperate for a woman to hold me just a moment, to hold me as Nonnie held me (without questions or explanations), yet unable to ask, needing probably my mother more than any other time or any other woman, I went instead to one of the bars and brought a woman back here to the apartment.

146

When she sat on the bed where Corette and I had loved, I burst into sobs and ran out into the street until I fell and nearly re-broke my arm. When I came back, she had gone. Her name was Claudii. She had dark eyes. She left a word-sketch of herself in my head: Your boots fall, *Clump! Clump!* by my bed and you fall, *Whump!*, into my pillows stretching your square ang-u-lar-i-ty out open to me. And the face you call your own wears no particular affection. There is no sister in your heart. I wonder if you will say, "Come here to me," as I wish you would, as I hope you won't. Or will you just lay there, in my pillows, looking at me looking back at you?

Berrigan's Journal — September 16

A re-stocking of groceries impends for our survival. I can't stall it off any longer. But to go out and have to talk to people, even the checker, seems impossible. I'm empty of words, sentiments, ideas, small talk: I need an escort who will translate for me. But who?

Paloma comes and puts her head in my lap. Hoby pokes her head over the bedroom railing. She barks, then joins us, her tail whirring, her toe-nails clicking all the way down the stairs. I have not been a fair companion to these, my best of friends, and now they offer to be my buffers against the world of people. How uncluttered their loyalty! So I accept their protection, and will brave a venture to the supermarket.

In this huge barn full of cans that glint from the shelves and oranges with winking navels, I watched mothers race up and down the aisles with restless babies kicking the carts. Their thoughts seemed tangible to me. "We must get home before the cake falls, before the towels mildew, before the soap operas unwind out of view!" I want to stop them and say, *"What are these concerns? Corette is dead. She'll never paint again."*

But their faces wouldn't change, anymore than Claudii's face. They go on racing, their cart wheels spinning, and Claudii goes on dropping her boots on the floor whenever there are pillows to fall into. Blank surfaces, these uncovered faces, ignoring death. Or are they death? More of death's voice, like the guns at the funeral?

Clutching my sacks, I finally finished and reached the car, gloriously relieved that the two pink noses poking out of the windows belonged to my boogie babies. They are always glad to see me, bear my rage without disloyalty, and share their warm bellies as comfort in sleep.

It felt okay to be out, not at the spaceage crazy-cart garage, but just out of the apartment and the weight of its memories. Yet I was glad to be heading back; despite the pain, Corette's comforting is there as nowhere else.

Berrigan's Journal — September 23

Dust and cobwebs and scratchy sounds of roaches shifting in nests compelled me out of my lethargy today, into furious scrubbing, sweeping, mopping, and the eventual re-arranging of some of Corette's things. I tried to ignore what I was doing, fought hard a tightness in me, a voice saying, "It's time to pack up a dead artist's easel, time to put the costumes of love into storage."

I passed the bowl of letters at least a hundred times but still cannot open them. But that must follow, if not today or tomorrow, soon. It is a neglect of Corette in a way, this shutting out of the feelings of her friends sent as memorial to her and in support of me. I must call or write ValJean also, and see Billy. Perhaps it's time to hold them now, as we didn't or couldn't do earlier. Surely that cannot be as painful as Claudii's blank face in my bedroom. It's just that I feel so voiceless, so unable to be with anyone after Corette, who surrounded me with fairness, compassion, her mild-wild adventures, her patient gentle love. Everything else seems rough, and eventually trite in comparison. Is aloneness better?

Berrigan's Journal – September 26
At 8:00 A.M., I awoke to the phone as clarion, but stumbled to answer it.

"You bes come outa dat ivory tower, girl, and let me boogie you back into dah mainstream! Lotta folks worrin' boutcha! Wondrin' whetha you still alive and well up dere!"

"Oh Billy, it's so good to hear from you!"

Billy was so glad I had actually answered the phone that he wanted to come right over and cook me a "soul breakfast" and catch me up on the latest in Charleston. But I'm not ready for ham-hocks and grits by a long shot, nor for warmed over gay gossip. Not that I'm not sympathetic with Billy and grateful for his repeated and persistent efforts to bring me out of myself since the funeral. But I can't be his new Corette, and I think he'd be willing for that. So we just talked on the phone. He's leaving Charleston this Friday for Atlanta to go visit two friends; I got their story in detail. It's an age-old one, about two straight men who fell in love and have been almost crucified for it by well-meaning family and friends.

"That's what happens when men love men!" I said.

"Only when they kiss and tell!" Billy quipped. "They need me now, though," he went on, "to fend off their own depression about all these pressures, and of course, to tell them it's quite alright for them to be in love."

"You can do that," I told him, *"better than anyone I know."*

"Anyone, except maybe Corette." We both paused, still feeling the shock of her absence. "You take care now, Berrigan, till I get back, you heah? Don't be crazy either. We got enough of a loss already. You find yourself standin' out somewhere thinkin' 'bout coppin' out, you just know Corette is three steps behind you. And she's gonna cuss your ass if you mess up! Anyway, I'd never forgive you and let me tell you, an Irish nigger with a grudge ain't nothin' to take lightly!"

"Have a gay old time in Atlanta, Billy. Leave your mark now! But please, leave a few of them still standing when you come back."

"Are you kiddin'? They all gonna be flat on their backs and grinnin' when I split. They gonna havetah take a vacation to get over me!"

When we hung up, I knew he'd told me something valuable: jumping off a bridge somewhere to join Corette in my own death would not be a win for either of us. Building the kind of bridge between myself and other people, as she always did with her genuineness and insight: that is the real win, the best direction I can take. I've been letting death steal my thoughts and put me at a distance from myself and Corette. It is time to stop paying homage to grief.

Berrigan's Journal — September 27

Another nightmare last night . . . my dream started with a lady who kept showing me photographs of all her dead relatives. Then I saw myself out on the street, sobbing, handing out pictures of Corette laid against a red velvet casket pillow. Finally in this vision a dyke walked up to me and said, "Do you think you're the only lesbian who ever lost her lover?"

This morning I am shakey, jumping at even familiar sounds in the apartment. Just as I was about to take a sip of tea, I distinctly heard a hammer pounding and the sound of a saw. I was hallucinating Corette and I building the staircase; how huggable she was in her carpenter's apron with a pencil stuck behind her ear. The hammer kept pounding louder and louder until I thought I could scream! Then it stopped.

Those sounds were me, trying to pound my way out of this concentration on death, putting my spirit and Corette's in agony. I have abandoned What Is for anger with fate about What Is No More and that is a death in itself, a staring into the slave pits and shutting out the messages coming from them. Corette never shut anyone out. In her praise, criticism, support, teasing, she chose the essential without a lot of flashy advertising or empty adjectives. How much she taught me!

I have resolved to open the mail. It is not fair to ignore the messages of our friends any longer. What was it Corette told me when I rode the bus in from Bingham? "Mourning is selfish. It wastes the present."

Berrigan's Journal — September 28

Despite my resolutions, I balked again at opening the mail and chose instead to take the dogs to the park. It would be impossible to explain what a help they've been, just having them around. They soothe what is angry in me, abiding my rule and wrath, knowing all and forgiving all. Without a gripe, they tolerate late meals, late hours, often ungentle caress, and a muddy backyard. They never pout, these boogie babies. Corette picked them because they always have smiles ready for any circumstance. They are my poetry when I cannot write. And they are welcome when I reject everyone else, including myself. Hoby licks the inside of my hand . . . and makes it seem possible to endure without our Boogie Mama.

Berrigan's Journal — September 30

At last, a poem! Mulling over the problem of Billy's friends in Atlanta, and the plight of all homosexuals dealing with society, with their own adjustments, with the barrage of ignorance that generalizes all of us, I came up with an epic verse. When I finished and looked around the apartment, hearing its silence, I felt Corette move in my heart, knew I had made a step out of death's shadow.

Berrigan's Journal — October 5

All the letters are opened, all those odes of sympathy for Corette, for me, Corette's lover, for us, woman-lovers married by good karma. The wishes spread out of each small card like a protective fan, coming from sisters, friends, mothers. I have opened them and stopped their noise in the bowl in the hall, have let out all their mournful mantras, their touchy goodbyes and bloody tears. For the brief time that their white square shapes were spread out on my knees, a familiar gnawing ache stole over me: the ache left in my life by the male-mantis Death, the unprisonable thief who traded an ache to me for Corette. Corette, as she used to be: on a wharf making love with me, as little huffing noises traveled back and forth between our mouths.

Refusing to worship death any longer, I folded all the squares back up and dusted Corette's books, tied up our letters in a piece of blue yarn, and wrapped her paintings.

I have called Evelyn, who came to help me with final details. Shoulder to shoulder, we packed up the pieces of Berrigan in Charleston.

Finally where we lived our love-life, our day-night womanworld, is empty, though not deserted. Corette's signature is here and always will be, in the dust in the couch pillows, in the paint spots and clay clumps left on the porch, in the sun pools where smiles she smiled here echo, and in a sigh from the bedroom platform where all our dreams came true.

Oh my Pollyana, you are taking me back to Bingham again, even though I wish for a Pegasus to fly me from my desperations and to you, of course, if it were possible. I would rather be with you, away from the countryside we'll be crossing soon, where mortal war is waged on Interstate and where abandoned women are taxed for taking in more than ten abandoned cats to feed.

Maybe it's better that you aren't here, Corette, even for me and my needs and our love. Not here to see these things, to hear the slave pit voices anymore. But I'm carrying you inside of me for good luck, and I promise most of my thoughts carry you somewhere in them. I promise!

150

Chapter 10

Back in Bingham without energy for defensiveness, Berrigan went to her parents' home, as sanctuary. Not that safe, comfortable world which she had made with Corette in Charleston, not that which she had made with Evelyn in side-by-side Army cots, but *home*: to the blood root, where any personal intrusions would be careful, even protective. Wearing the death of a friend on her sleeve, a lover undeclared, Berrigan knew her parents would withdraw from the old games, at least long enough for her to rest and restore herself.

She was not wrong, knew them even for all that they did not understand in her. As plans were made and re-made for Evelyn's wedding ceremony, Berrigan worked at being calm and her parents gave her space for that without question. She did not fail to notice their exchanged silent messages, though, nor stop to wonder if she was the topic of their muffled midnight conversations. Now was a time for them to come through for her, and they did not fail, though worry was evident in their faces. Once the strain broke through, manifested in a scenario Berrigan did not observe. Her mother was standing at the bottom of the stairs leading up to Berrigan's room, where the gravelly sound of old 45-records had passed for hours with Berrigan absorbed in nostalgia from Bingham High. Her mother almost called up to her, "Come down, honey, and let's talk. Are you all right?" Her hand touched the railing for a moment; she started that first step up to reach her daughter, but turned at the last minute to pick up a broom and brush off the porch, whisking her own doubts and questions away with the leaves.

Letting her thoughts dangle, Berrigan stayed in, except for a nightly walk on the BC college campus with the dogs. Evelyn called frequently, urging her to go out and keeping her posted on the latest agenda for the wedding. But still she kept her days slow, almost langorous, giving her attention to the dogs and watching the afternoon soap operas. Conversations with her parents were tenuous, fragile. They were all learning a new status with one another.

With the punchbowl secured and the minister alerted, the ceremony was finally organized and arrived without fanfare except for the quickness behind Evelyn's eyes, her anticipation signaled to Berrigan early in the day when they met at BJ's.

"Do I look like a bride?" Evelyn asked.

"Uh huh. A little green around the edges."

Berrigan grinned and they clacked beer mugs in a familiar toast. The world was full of unspoken significance, it seemed, everyone all silence about their feelings: Berrigan of her own for Corette, her parents withholding their questions, and now Evelyn as she reached across the table to take her friend's hand, saying with her look, "My friend, you will always have a space in my life."

Then she retreated, masking her emotions in a monologue of disgust about the bothersome conventions of getting married, most notably her mother's incessant fussing over every detail.

"I feel more like this is my first prom than my wedding!"

"Only in this case, you don't have to endure that agonizing quandary: will he kiss me at the door!"

"Berrigan, I can't believe you don't think Daniel and I are both virgins!"

"Come on, Evelyn! There's something suspicious about you wanting to wear lavender instead of the traditional white gown. And you never asked me where to get a diaphragm."

"I wasn't sure you'd know! After all, it's been a long time since your raving heterosexual phase!"

"Thank goodness I got over that!"

"As for my color scheme, I figured you'd rejoice. Isn't lavender your color?"

"Sure, but you can borrow it for today. You'll be beautiful. But not as much as when you wear your sweatshirt!"

They both thought of their day at the farm and laughed, leaving to drive to Evelyn's apartment. At her door, Berrigan told her, *"I've got the rings. See you at 8:30. You do remember which church, don't you?"*

"Come in just a sec, Berrigan. I've got a surprise for you."

"If I don't leave now to get ready, I won't make it on time!"

"Oh just *one second*, ole skeptical you! Come on!"

Evelyn was plaintive enough to convince Berrigan. Once inside, Evelyn announced she wanted to model her trousseau.

"I know you didn't want to go along to help me pick this out, Berrigan, so here's an exclusive chance for a sneak preview."

Before Berrigan could protest, Evelyn had rushed into the next room in a flourish of excitement. Berrigan was about half mad at her for her insensitivity; she was sad enough to see her friend on the road to Hartford domesticity. As she was about to decide to skip out on the entire ceremony, Evelyn yelled to her, "Ready?"

"Ready," Berrigan replied glumly.

Evelyn stepped into the room and Berrigan gasped with surprise. For there stood the bride-on-the-brink in an elegant lavender pantssuit, gorgeous but blatantly contemporary. She twirled in it, and the light soft material billowed.

"Speechless?"

Berrigan nodded.

"Listen, Mom can have this wedding as much as she wants but there are some things about it that must be entirely my own. This is one of them."

Evelyn did another twirl.

"I love this!"

"So do I. Of course."

"And why do I need a veil? This is one woman getting married without covering up her head!"

"Evelyn, you're crazy! And I love you for it!"

They ran to each other, eager for hugs. They were both shakey with all the expectations of the day, reassured by their old comfortable friendship.

"I've got to run or your best person will be late."

"I know. My parents will be here from the church soon."

Berrigan hurried for the door, but turned back to Evelyn.

"Who'd a thunk it? I'm proud of you."

"And I of you."

Berrigan chose to walk to the church rather than ride with Evelyn or her parents. She stopped about half a block from the building, noticed it dressed in October frost, its surrounding trees a solemn fall choir. Some early guests were arriving, their car doors breaking the damp late-autumn quiet. Evelyn drove up then, with her younger sister Claire. As Berrigan walked closer but still out of their sight, she heard their voices, twenty-ish and gay. They ran into the church, burgeoned with boxes. More guests followed in their American array of blue serge, grey pinstripe, here and there a dress with an orange slash of color. All the shoes were worn down at the heel.

Once inside the church, the smells of religion oozed heavy throughout: the pungeance of fresh paint, tired wood scents from stored pews, dust heavy in sagging curtains. Coughs that once broke through prayers echoed ghostly. Berrigan sighed and listened to the hollow sounds in the hallways, satcheled her own stresses for her friend's nuptial.

Berrigan made two stops before the parade down the altar: one to reassure the groom and one to secure the bride. Seeking Daniel, she spied him in the tearful clutches of Mrs. Walker, who was weeping last minute instructions to him. Mr. Walker shook Daniel's hand and then steered his wife towards the front row seats in the sanctuary. Berrigan waited unobtrusively at the far end of the hall. Watching the Walkers go, Daniel leaned against the wall and brushed a passive hand through his thin hair.

"Is the groom trembly?"

Daniel looked up, startled by her voice.

"Yes . . . no . . ." He laughed. "It's sort of like when I play a solo. At first, there's terror. But then when the notes start to flow I'm done before I know it. I've played a gorgeous melody."

"Is Mr. Walker making things rough on you?"

"Oh no. He's being very kind. He didn't even wear his 'Mayor of Hartford' button. I think he's just trying to get his wife through this."

Suddenly Daniel began searching his pockets frantically.

"The rings. Where are the rings? What have I done with them?"

"Did you forget? I've got the rings. That's what I'm for, remember?"

He relaxed with a sheepish grin.

"Well, I better go drag the tigress from her lair. See you at the altar!"

Dressing in the nursery, Evelyn's back was to the door as Berrigan entered. The sight of naked shoulders stung Berrigan, sent her for a moment reeling back to Corette and that most precious touch, those most precious hours. Berrigan shook away the memory, trying to smile. Evelyn, turning at Berrigan's entry, asked, "Well?"

"Slick!"

"Oh god, Claire, I've left Grandma's locket in the car! Will you get it for me? Berrigan, will you help me with one last thing? Will you brush my hair out?"

Pulling the brush through Evelyn's hair, golden against her lavender blouse, Berrigan could feel their friendship: soft, fragrant, a light shadow on their shoulders. Neither woman said anything, both of them fighting a pervading wash of sentiment. Then they both started to speak at once.

"My god, I wish I had a beer!"

"I should have sneaked one in!"

"No, no! We'd both have been struck by thunderbolts! So how do I look? Portrait of the Hartford snob as Bride Beautiful?"

Evelyn posed, pointing one toe. Her hand on her hip, she shook her hair.

"You need your nose up just a little higher. That's it."

"Christ, this stuff is ridiculous. But at least I'm not corseted into one of those white lace cages. It reminds me of Victorian costumes. I wonder how those women ever made love?"

Berrigan grinned and raised her eyebrows knowingly.

"Never mind! I can imagine your answer to that! Have you seen Daniel? Has my mother completely terrorized him?"

"No. He's holding his own. Has your mother resigned herself to the idea of my not being a bridesmaid?"

"No, she's still upset. We went round and round about it again last night. She kept telling me it wasn't too late to call up Dora and Mickey. It must be a great burden for my debutante cousins, always keeping a closet of formals on stand-by."

"What'd she say about the pantssuit?"

"At first I thought we'd have to give her first aid! She was fit to

154

be tied. I got this grandiose lecture on the value of tradition and of course, she blamed you for all my 'unnaturally independent' tendencies! I loved that! Thank god for Berrigan, I secretly gloried. But finally, Dad came in and even as the all-proper mayor, he couldn't resist how I look in this outfit. Besides, I saved him a lot of money! And he does recognize the power of the dollar, especially when he can spend it! Not that he's cutting corners; I mean, really, all those tiers of designer cake: every layer should be made of gold! All this expense for one event: sometimes I think it's completely stupid."

An organ chord sounded just as Claire returned. Evelyn put on the delicate gold locket.

"Ready?"

They looked at each other, wavering another minute together, with a mixture of fear and joy.

"Now's your last chance to escape with me and live as beer bums and vagabonds forever!"

Berrigan was being facetious but reassuring. Evelyn shook her head yes, and then no. Hugging again and giggling, *"Look out for your orchid!"*, they both opened the door to the sanctuary as the wedding march proceeded full swing.

Tears wet the maternal cheeks after the ceremony and reception as Evelyn stretched out her arm, letting the bridal bouquet cartwheel down into the crowd of women gathered on the church steps. Someone caught the flowers, a woman Berrigan did not know. She came up from the crowd of eager maidens, her face broken open with the thrill of prophesy.

"I'm next," she cried, "I'm next!"

Before there was time to sprinkle them with rice, Daniel and Evelyn were gone, trundled all trunks and clothes-on-hangers in Daniel's sturdy new beetle-car, a wedding present from his parents.

"Daniel will have a heck of a time getting all the shave cream off the windows," Claire mused. "I almost hated to mess up his new car."

* * * * * *

October 30 (Nearly November!)
Happy Halloween!

Dearest ValJean,

I know at the very beginning of this letter that I have no right to ask your forgiveness of my obvious neglect, but I promise you, it's been purely circumstantial! Between the time I closed the apartment in Charleston and now, I've been busy marrying off a close friend, Evelyn Walker. And then there's been the readjustment to Bingham and to my own constant introspections. And frankly, the worry of how to form my thoughts to you, what to write in sorting

155

through the barrage of images, memory, confusion, and pain since June 25. We were all without words after the funeral, and it is all still too close, bringing frequent tears. But remembering Corette's optimism helps. I have realized how she managed to loan me my own strength.

I speak of readjusting to Bingham but mean more clearly of forgetting Charleston and a lifestyle so different there. And of course, I haven't lived in my parents' home for many years, and that is not now easy. Mom has been full of furtive concern for me since I came back, which she casts at me out of the corners of her eyes. But in her defense, she's just trying to be subtle and I do appreciate that. Dad, on the other hand, is restless with worry now that Evelyn is married and gone and I have not shown any signs of searching for a beau of my own. In that too, though, is a well meant protection and I know what is foremost in his mind: he does not want me to be *alone*. Unfortunately, I cannot unload my heart to them so that I would be more relaxed in their company. How can I ever end up alone after loving Corette?

But now that I am here in Bingham and have shut off frequent panicky urges to pack and fly off to destinations unknown, what do I do? Several Saturdays ago, wandering in the shops on the edge of the campus, I came upon a small one called "Shop Desiderata": full of handicrafts, paintings, pots, beadwork, rope weaving. As I browsed through canvases by the local painters, low and behold, "Artist and Dogs of Calais" was there as well, slightly apart from the others and obviously more regal. I couldn't believe that distinct *V.H.* slashed in the corner. I stared at the picture, seeing both you and Corette in the face of the woman in your painting. Fortune must have drawn me to find your picture in that shop!

The woman who owns the store is going to Australia to study and wants to sell it with most of the present stock intact, as well as a small apartment in the back. It would be a perfect place to put up some of Corette's paintings and more of your own. With more exposure, I have no doubt you'd sell, even though sometimes it takes awhile to flush out the art connoisseurs in a place the size of Bingham.

So I've decided to talk to my friendly banker about a loan to buy the shop. I've already arranged with Jacqueline, the present owner, to read her financial records. She says the profit is liveable. She really hasn't made the time for improvements in display, advertising, etc. But it's her approach that won me. She says she takes only single originals of anything displayed for sale and is fair on her commission to the artists.

"This shop has been like a cause with me, but it takes a dedication for which I no longer have the energy."

Her biggest initial fight was to avoid her space becoming a tourist trap or "head shop" since it's right off campus and gets some student trade. Thank god the place didn't reek of incense!

Of course, all my plans presuppose a liberty for which I want your approval: that you don't mind if I show Corette's paintings. It's about time she got her exhibit! In my previous short note to you, included with those financial and insurance papers I sent, I mentioned that I wanted to keep her sketchbook. If I get my wish, soon we'll sit down together and appreciate all the drawings. But I hope not sending it with her other things was not a slight to you. I don't know how to explain it, but I just felt they were drawn for me, as a gift she didn't get time to share. As for her paintings, they await your instructions for storing or shipping or hanging in "Shop Desiderata!"

It seems I've been fighting living in Bingham for the last few years, and now I'm not sure if it wasn't just my fear that I couldn't be happy without anonymity and "stretching room." But that space is here as much as it was with you and Corette in the studio in Calais. It's just that before, I turned all the externals about my parents and my past at the college into an unfounded "hometown paranoia." Maybe the trouble with thinking "you can never go home again" is that we expect home to be the one place that doesn't change. But just as I am only a remnant of my former self as I grow and learn, so is Bingham re-painted: the doors of the houses in my neighborhood, my parents mellowing and becoming more willing to let me be, any memory of me at the college fading into a moldy records room. And so finally home is not a place I visit hesitantly, wary of shadowed expectations.

In closing, please know that my thoughts are with you often, as I envision that warm cavern of the studio and you at work: your head cocked to one side in contemplation, paint splatters on your jeans and sneakers.

We share a bond no one else, not even Billy, can understand or join us in: the life and times of Corette, the wonder of who and what she was. I believe women can know each other deeply, sharing their mutual strength and beauty. This we truly gained from and gave to Corette.

I await news from you, hope your painting is going well. Oh! Also enclosed are two poems, my latest efforts now that I've risen from the lethargy of escape and hope I am coping again. The one on Picasso is for you. The one about Corette I hold in my hands like a prayer or a worry stone, reciting to myself when I am shakey.

With love,
Berrigan

* * * * * *

Corral Pablo
Calais, Vermont
November 7

Dear friend Berrigan,
How good to hear from you! Your letter was cheery greeting

157

today after an all-night painting binge I used to submerge a rush of grief. These are less frequent now, but I admit they completely sweep me over. I was so used to putting out my hand and Corette's being there to take it, offer a joke, or one of her special insights. Over these years, my daughter has been my best friend. And now it's a hard pattern to grow out of, especially against my will. Captain Jack has tried very hard to be an unimposing comfort, and Billy's letters are chocked-full of supportiveness, disguised of course, "in best jive."

Your contacts are especially appreciated by me because I believe you were closer to Corette than any of us; it was never a connection I could be jealous of, considering how it lighted up both of you, loosened your best selves. And so, knowing she was happy right up to the last moment offers important relief. Then there is the you who emerges in your poems, in your letters, in some vibrant spiritual message to me across our miles. Never think I don't love you except in relation to Corette; I know your singular self as well.

The two poems you sent in your recent letter were powerful. Our dear master Picasso would have been honored to read his, chuckling "how droll," no doubt! The more concise one for Corette reveals more to me with each reading. Like her, it releases its truth in small doses. Your words capture her in a familiar pose.

In all reassurance, let me say that the way you managed to collect Corette's things in Charleston saved me a large measure of pain. Wrapping her canvases and taking them with you to Bingham surely served to protect them better than trying to ship them here. Masterpieces have been lost that way! Mail service seems to have no awareness of the value of art! And of course I have no objection to your keeping the sketchbook; we'll share it together soon. It's a date! Sending the other things on to me released me from sorting and sifting through a loved one's ashes. I am immensely grateful to you for that.

Now to the topic I have foremost on my mind! In my trust, I have a sizeable fund Corette's father left her but which she rarely used. It would make me very happy if this money could help you in securing the shop you wrote me about, if this would not seem a breech of your independence on the project. You might think of it as her contribution to a venture I know she would have undertaken with you wholeheartedly. It's up to you, but however you decide to act on the financial source, you have my full approval and personal encouragement to display Corette's paintings.

By way of your desire to create a living memory to Corette, I am touched in a way impossible for me to relate to you. We share our grief on a deep level. Perhaps we both lost our one true love when Corette died.

If I ever release any of the canvases I've recently completed, count on at least four for yourself. They are better than "Artist and

Dogs of Calais." Oh Berrigan, I hope the shop goes! I am so excited for you because the shop sounds like just the niche for you, where you can be surrounded with creativity.

Eagerly, I anticipate further developments on all of this. Call me collect! And of course, I better get an invitation to the grand opening! Do be well, sweet friend; I think of you often, stopping at the canvas mid-stroke to remember our walks in the field together, you genuinely hoping to be good for Corette. How lucky you both were, we all were!

Back to the painting now, with my new commissions for you as inspiration!

Best love,
ValJean

* * * * * *

Berrigan's Journal — November 20

With Evelyn back from honeymooning as key volunteer to help me in moving, I embark on making "Shop Desiderata" a reality: for Corette and as my home, a private centered space for continuing the growth of that most exotic strain of psyche— Berrigan!

Taking it skeptically, my parents offer good wishes and frowns simultaneously, trying to do their duty to fairness and yet trusting more their own judgment that I should *not* try this. I have made my explanations to them, can give it no more time in words. I can no longer make their adjustment to my life for them, nor be here for them except as my own person, a fond visitor to their values. For all that we love about each other, we must now offer mutual release. If only I could give them ValJean's letter. Would it allay their fears, reassure them I will be all right? It might let them know that daughters who are woman-lovers will not turn to stone and perish in hell if their honesty is revealed.

Jacqueline was ecstatic that her efforts with the shop will be turned over to someone she considers "worthy and serious." She left me a potted palm as her welcoming gift. With a small bank loan and Corette's fund, I am in good shape with no debilitating payments to make.

Berrigan's Journal — November 21

In the clutter of boxes and cartons, with the scents of change in the air, Hoby and Paloma are candid, lounging here and there on tops of things to be rearranged. They scurry when I shoo them off; their eyes are a little cautious, questioning. Tonight in the apartment behind the shop, alone in our place at last, I gathered their warm, soft-furred selves into my arms, my lap full of their nimble legs, to explain it all to them.

Staring into the darkened shop, its silence broken only when the wind strokes a crystal chime, I could hear the time of my past throbbing, hear it ticking like seconds reborn, memories brought into being again. Of course it was Corette's face I saw in the dark, felt and heard again how it was to fall into the soft hot flesh of her, to that mouth of hers that purred over me. There was never enough time for us, lounging naked together, trading passions and theory between our sheets.

Time . . . there was never enough time for loving, sleeping tucked chin-to-chin, talking endlessly into every topic we thought of so that we might know where all the bases touched and feelings overlapped. We had to sandwich our "us" into a small space . . . it brings the tears, this cheat.

If it is true that we came together as Corette said, from karmic centuries as lovers, then we had already had much of our time together. I only wish I remembered those eras too, had not become aware in just the final round.

How she gave me my answers! Corette, who arrived mid-dream to my midnight ravings. Bleary-minded, with aching eyes, I gained sight of her: her alabaster back, her silver breasts, her total vision rising out of the parched coma that I had slipped into. Ah woman, you have blown full my ravaged wings so I could fly out of darkness!

I have flown out of darkness and have chosen my own dreams. Perhaps that is something Corette prided in me. Even through the raging rhetoric of Syru, I could not adopt her dream. It was not my answer to seek myself in Oregon with Jaye and Trudy. That community was their dream, as was Corette's "Fireseed", Linda's social reign, Mac's conquering business boogeymen. Now I sit inside the space of "Shop Desiderata," glimpsing my dream at last.

I arrive before my Woolworth's mirror with Corette's face in my mind. And yet I see my own face, loving its lines, it dark spaces where the loneliness shows. Behind my eyes rest my own dreams. This shop is my stopping-off place, my home for my Boogie Babies and the memory of their Boogie Mama. What delightful friends are these dogs Corette and I had together, and what a delightful place to tinker is the shop. I can step bare-footed over lounging dogs to arrange the gourd-and-acorn sculptures Jaye and Trudy sent, push up a corner of a tilted painting, redrape a bronze nude. Corette and I are cheering in this space in joyous voices only I can hear: "See ya later, alligator! After awhile, crocodile!" "Ho hum a holiday, home at last and settled in!"

Like sails that dip and rise, baptised in a new spring on the sea, I am purged, hull cleaned, my barnacles like grudges dissolved. Love flaps hard against my grief and pain, bids me come-about and catch a free wind.

OTHER PUBLICATIONS OF THE NAIAD PRESS

THE LATECOMER, by Sarah Aldridge. A Novel. 107 pages.
ISBN   0-930044-00-2 $4.50

TOTTIE, by Sarah Aldridge. A Novel. 181 pages.
ISBN   0-930044-01-0 $4.50

CYTHEREA'S BREATH, by Sarah Aldridge. A Novel. 240 pages.
ISBN   0-930044-02-9 $5.00

SPEAK OUT, MY HEART, by Robin Jordan. A Novel. 148 pages.
ISBN   0-930044-03-7 $4.00

A WOMAN APPEARED TO ME, by Renée Vivien, Translated from the French by Jeannette H. Foster. A Novel, with Introduction by Gayle Rubin. xli, 90 pages.
ISBN   0-930044-06-1 $4.00

LESBIANA, by Barbara Grier. Book reviews from *THE LADDER*. iv, 309 pages.
ISBN   0-930044-05-3 $5.00

LOVE IMAGE, by Valerie Taylor. A Novel. 168 pages.
ISBN   0-930044-08-8. $4.50

THE MUSE OF THE VIOLETS, by Renée Vivien. Translated from the French by Margaret Porter and Catharine Kroger. Poetry. xiv, 70 pages.
ISBN   0-930044-07-X $4.00

ALL TRUE LOVERS, by Sarah Aldridge. A Novel. 292 pages.
ISBN   0-930044-10-X $6.75

ALSO OBTAINABLE FROM THE NAIAD PRESS:

THE LESBIAN IN LITERATURE, A Bibliography, Compiled by Gene Damon, Jan Watson, and Robin Jordan. 96 pages.
ISBN   0-930044-04-5 $7.00

THE NAIAD PRESS, INC.
7800 WESTSIDE DRIVE
WEATHERBY LAKE, MISSOURI 64152

Mail Orders Welcome
Please include 15% Postage